Dr. Jeffrey T. Rainey

PARALYSIS *in the* PEW

Treating the Malady of Spiritual Quiescence

Scripture taken from the King James Version of the Bible.

WestBow Press books may be ordered through booksellers or by contacting:

WestBow Press
A Division of Thomas Nelson & Zondervan
1663 Liberty Drive
Bloomington, IN 47403
www.westbowpress.com
1 (866) 928-1240

ISBN: 978-1-5127-5765-1 (sc)
ISBN: 978-1-5127-5766-8 (hc)
ISBN: 978-1-5127-5764-4 (e)

Library of Congress Control Number: 2016915713

Print information available on the last page.

WestBow Press rev. date: 09/20/2016

DEDICATION

To the memory of my father,
the late Elder Walter D. Rainey Sr.,
who instilled, inspired, and illustrated the importance of information.
My accomplishments are the harvest from the seeds he sowed.

To my mother, Emma S. Rainey,
who has been a permanent strength, a passionate supervisor,
and a proud support for her pentavalent son.

To my wife, Carolyn Suzette, who has been the "be" of my being.
She has been beneath me to balance me. She
has been behind me to boost me.
She has been beside me to brace me.

To my children, Caryn Seleta and Carmen Suzette,
who have been caring, committed contributors
to my calling and to this cause.

To my siblings and to my relatives by marriage,
for stimulating me, supporting me, and
strengthening me toward this success.

To my Church family, the Christian Union Primitive Baptist Church,
for their patience, their prompting, and
their prayers during this pursuit.

TABLE OF CONTENTS

LIST OF TABLES

ACKNOWLEDGMENTS

Success is not without support. I am happy, honored, and humbled for the help from the persons God positioned on my pilgrimage.

I acknowledge the three people who gave me letters of recommendations: Dr. Oscar L. Montgomery Sr., pastor of Union Hill Primitive Baptist Church, Huntsville, Alabama, who has shepherded me, steered me, and shaped me as a pastor and a preacher; Elder Timothy M. Rainey, pastor of Indian Creek Primitive Baptist Church, Huntsville, Alabama, who is my blood brother, my faith friend, and a spiritual standard and who has been a mentor, a model, and a motivator for my ministry; and Dr. George T. Brooks, pastor of St. James Missionary Baptist Church, Nashville, Tennessee, who has provided his prudence, his persuasion, and his promotion in this pursuit.

I acknowledge the faculty and the staff of Faith Evangelical Seminary, who have exposed me to materials, educated me in methods, and equipped me for ministry.

I acknowledge Dr. Bruce Bronoske, my advisor, who has helped me, handled me, and held me with a heart and a hand of humility.

I also acknowledge Dr. Michael J. Adams, president of Faith Evangelical College and Seminary, who has nurtured me, nudged me, and navigated me by name, by nature, and by need to my degree destination.

Above all, I acknowledge God for gifting me, guiding me, and guarding me to this goal.

Chapter 1

INTRODUCTION: THE PROBLEM STATED AND DEFINED

The Church is an institution with which many want to be identified, but it is not an institution with which many want to be involved. Many may come, but few are committed. Involvement is what induces, initiates, and inspires our interest, our intellect, our incentive, our investment, and our increase. I firmly believe that every person has a part to play in the overall divine program—a mandate to meet in membership. Each individual has an incentive for involvement in the institution. Herbert W. Byrne summarizes the situation.

> Major denominations in this country have many names of people who do not attend services or participate in the program of the Church. As far back as 1978, George Gallup in his study entitled *Unchurched Americans* shows that at least 61 million American adults were not members of any Church. The same study reported that many Americans did not think Church membership and attendance were important in being Christian. In 1980 Gallup and Poling, in their book *The Search for America's Faith* (Abingdon, 1980, 80), reported that unchurched people are just as religious as those who attend Church. The Princeton

> Religious Research Center in their publication Emerging Trends indicated in 1982 that 67% of U.S. adults claimed to be Church members, and 41% attended some service in any given week. This improved to 73% and 37% respectively as reported in another study by the same people for 1983. It must be pointed out, however, that in some denominations many of these people would be classified as inactive.[1]

I have adopted in my spirit, as well as in my service, the recruiting slogan of the United States Army: "Be All That You Can Be." By *all*, the author means "complete," "total," and "whole." Additionally, my desire for my congregation is complete cooperation—the totality of the people taking part, and the whole working. I hope that this passion for parishioners' participation in the divine program is not my own alone. Someone else *had* to be bearing this burden for believers—a desire that they be busy within the body of Christ. For that reason, I have aspired to acquire the actions, the agendas, and the approaches of other assemblies—seeking answers, antidotes, and applications for this worthy ambition.

In Scripture, the Church is often symbolized in three metaphors: as a building (2 Peter 2:5), as a bride (Eph. 5:25–27), and as a body (1 Cor. 12:27). In these comparisons, the building is often used to represent the structure and the stability of the Church; the bride is often used to represent the submissiveness and security of the Church; and the body is often used to represent the service and the support of the Church. For the purpose of this study, the image focus will be upon the body. The human body is everything that makes up, well, you. The basic parts of the human body are the head, neck, torso, arms, and legs. Bodies consist of a number of biological systems that carry out specific functions necessary for everyday living.[2] The body has been referred to

---

1. Herbert W. Byrne, *Reclaiming Inactive Church Members* (Bloomington, IN: Trafford Publishing, 2006), 11–12.
2. Rachael Rettner, "The Human Body: Anatomy, Facts and Functions," *Live Science*, May 2013, http://www.livescience.com/37009-human-body.html.

as the “marvelous machine” because of its amazing ability to move, to maneuver, and to function in remarkable ways; these same remarkable attributes are reflective of attributes and capabilities of the body of Christ when it is healthy, harmonious, and whole.

It is the full participation and proper functioning of each member that brings about the fulfillment of the body in its God-designed function. People often think of themselves as total, complete, or whole. When they go to the doctor and receive a good report, they speak of being in “perfect” health. When they eat right, exercise regularly, and get enough rest, they speak of being in “perfect” shape. When they complete a task without a hitch, they speak of having done a “perfect” job. Everyone wants his or her body to fulfill all of its intended functions—to work perfectly. Now, imagine the body of Christ with flesh and form. What if the body was not functioning properly? One can only imagine trying to lift something with an arm that is not functioning properly. One can only imagine trying to perform intricate, detailed work with the hand not functioning properly; to run when one leg is not functioning properly or to stand when one foot is not functioning properly. It would make any daily task difficult—if not impossible. A simple activity would become a struggle. When a body part is not functioning as designed, the whole body is affected—it is disadvantaged. When one member is not functioning as designed, the body can neither perform nor produce to its fullest potential or capacity.

Each true believer in the Lord Jesus Christ is a member of the body of Christ—the Church. And the Church has been given the role of proclaiming the message, performing the ministry, and promoting the mission of Christ. When each member is present, participating, and persistent, the program of the Church and of its Lord is productive. However, when members of the body are not functioning as designed, the body of Christ limps in her walk, lags in her work, and loses in her witness. The Church fails to fulfill her mission and function. This is what the author calls *functional paralysis*.

Luke 7:36–50 tells the story of Jesus attending a dinner at the house of Simon, the Pharisee. While Jesus was eating, a woman of the street entered, and, sparing no expense, she performed a celebratory act over Him. Jesus responded to her attending to Him by saying, "She loved much" (Luke 7:47). The phrase "she loved much" was Jesus's explanation for her extravagant and tender, caring expression toward Him. Jesus implied that this love was a heart reaction—a response to her full awareness and appreciation of her acquittal. By contrast, many believers are ignorant of the full penalty of their sin, the full price of their salvation, or the privilege they hold as saints of the Most High. If they were aware, their love would be reflected in their life and service. They too would "love much."

This passage in Luke 7 addresses a question over which I have agonized for some time. Why is it that some members are involved in the mission and ministry of the church while others remain idle? Why is it that some members are interested while others remain indifferent? Why is it that some members are increasing while others are insipid? There were at least two people in the house of Simon the Pharisee. Each had equal access to Jesus. One was serving, but the other was merely sitting. Both, however, were in the same house. The difference is *not* due to the following:

- **Lack of attendance.** Both Simon and the woman were present in the house. Each had the same opportunity to minister to the Master. Likewise, members who attend Church have the opportunity to serve and are available to both participate in and perform the ministries of the Church. While some do their parts, others choose not to.
- **Lack of awareness.** Both Simon and the woman knew the customs of the day. Custom dictated that when guests arrived, the host would wash their feet in a gesture of welcome, anoint them with oil in a gesture of respect, and kiss their brows in a gesture of affection. Church members are generally aware of the

various opportunities and their obligation to assist. While some do their parts, others choose not to participate.

- **Lack of ability.** Apparently, Simon and the woman were in adequate physical condition. There is no mention of any debilitation or disability that would render this service impossible. The work that needs to be done in the Church (done as unto the Lord) is within the general, physical, mental, and spiritual capacities of many within the congregation. Yet, some will put their hands to the plow while others will not lift a hand. Again, while some do their part, others do not.

Jesus says the difference is affection. Jesus said, "If ye love Me, keep My commandments" (John 14:15). An unknown composer of an African American spiritual titled "We Are Climbing Jacob's Ladder" penned in one stanza: "If you love Him, why not serve Him? Soldiers of the Cross." If each member functioned as he or she were gifted and intended, the body of Christ could perform to its fullest, divine potential.

The Problem Addressed by the Study

It was during a noticeable lapse in membership, member involvement, and activity when I became increasingly concerned with the following:

- Low attendance at worship
- A diminished appetite for the Word
- Little desire for the work of the Lord
- A weakening aversion to the things of the world
- A noticeable loss of desire to be a witness

Questions such as, *Why are current members not attending?* and *Why are prospective members not coming?* often dominated my thoughts. It is not pleasant preaching to empty pews. I grew up in a home where my parents wanted the family home at mealtime. We did not have the luxury of eating when we wanted or warming up food whenever we determined to eat. When it was dinnertime, everyone sat down together at the table to entreat the Father, engage in fellowship, embrace the family, and enjoy the food. It was a special time!

My earthly parents wanted the family at home to be together for mealtimes. So, too, the heavenly Father desires a full house. And though covering a number of divine appeals, this particular desire is reflected in the parable of the Great Supper in Luke 14: "And the lord said unto the servants, Go out into the highways and hedges, and compel them to come in, that My house may be filled" (Luke 14:23). The master of the feast did not want empty seats. He had prepared a great feast, and much food and drink was on hand. Without a full crowd, the food and drink would be wasted. Furthermore, without a full crowd, the master of the house would be dishonored and the splendor of the feast diminished.

Likewise, God is not excited when His house is not full. God is not pleased when family members are absent. God does not rejoice when the seats are empty. It is as if the Lord were saying, "Go, and get someone to sit in these seats. There are people who need to be here!" God wants a full house at mealtime; the Lord does not want empty seats. He wants everybody seated when the meal is ready to be served.

I then asked myself some hard questions: *Why should current members attend?* and *Why should prospective members come?* Someone has to invite them! Something has to inspire them and prove itself needful to them. So, the conclusion was drawn: God wants not only a full house but a focused house. People come when

- the purpose is clear,
- the people are compassionate,
- the policies are canonical,
- the programs are coordinated, and
- the practices are consistent.

When we lift the Master, we lure the masses. Jesus said, "And I, if I be lifted up from the earth, will draw all men unto Me" (John 12:32).

Beyond wanting a full house at mealtime and a focused house in the meantime, God wants a functioning house in the ministry. God does not want just attendees who are attracted *to* the Church, only. He wants us to be active *in* the Church. Being a Christian means caring about the life and the health of the body of Christ—the Church. It means caring what the Church is and what the Church should be, not simply that one belongs to the Church. The only way to lighten this load is to ask the Lord for laborers. For Jesus said, "Pray ye therefore the Lord of the harvest, that He will send forth laborers into His harvest" (Matt. 9:38). Jesus acknowledged the aggravation of being shorthanded at harvest time. "Then saith He unto His disciples, The harvest truly is plenteous, but the labourers are few" (Matt. 9:37). According to *Webster's New Collegiate Dictionary*, *shorthanded* is defined as "short of the regular or necessary number of people." Wherever there is a shortage, there is less productivity, a loss in profitability, and a limit to possibility.

The burden of the Church is not that it lacks having something specific to do. Quite the opposite is true. It holds a mandate; it has been given a mission by the Master. What it lacks is manpower. The Church has more work than workers. I submit that the Church has the highest of "unemployment" rates. It has too many believers who are not busy; too many Christians who are not committed; too many individuals who are idle; too many saints who are sitting. It is harvest time! The field is ripe, and we are shorthanded. As Jesus said, "The harvest is plenteous, but the laborers are few."

One of the fundamental reasons the world is in such poor condition physically, psychologically, and spiritually is that the harvest is plenteous, but much of the help is AWOL. "*The laborers are few.*" Few Christians and churches have the following:

- The insight—the ability to detect, discern, and define people's conditions

- The interest—they lack the care, the concern, and the compassion for the lost and hurting
- The involvement—they will not spend their time, talent, or treasure to help

Sadly, the Church and Christians are, in many ways, responsible for the world's present condition. Or, at the very least, the Church has not done her full, God-ordained part to mitigate the world's present decline. Remember, "If My people, which are called by My name, shall humble themselves, and pray, and seek My face, and turn from their wicked ways; then will I hear from heaven, and will forgive their sins, and will heal their land" (2 Chron. 7:14). In other words, if the Church would do what she has been called and commissioned to do, God would hear her supplications, cover her sins, and heal her sicknesses.

The Significance of the Problem

Current Church leaders are well aware of the eighty/twenty rule, which states that 20 percent of the membership does 80 percent of the work, while 80 percent of the members do 20 percent of the work. Thom S. Rainer suggests that many Church members have lost the biblical understanding of what it means to be a part of the body of Christ. Rainer says,

> Whenever a child is born, he or she automatically becomes a part of the universal family of human beings. But that child also needs to become a member of a specific family to receive nurture and care and grow up healthy and strong. The same is true spiritually. When you were born again, you automatically became a part of God's universal family, but you also need to become a member of a local expression of God's family.[3]

3. Rick Warren, *The Purpose Driven Life: What on Earth Am I Here For?* (Grand Rapids, MI: Zondervan, 2002), 136.

When we are in a family, we inherit roles and intimate relationships. Both come with responsibilities. In the human family, we are responsible for roles, for routines, and for respect. In the spiritual family, we are responsible for serving, for sharing, and for supporting. Responsibility comes with growth and maturity. No one expects a newborn to feed itself, walk on its own, or do things around the house. That comes with time, with teaching, and with training. So it is with us. When we are spiritually born again, we are not ready to lead a ministry, to teach a Bible study, or to counsel people. That comes with time, teaching, and training.

We go through the process because we do not want to become grown without growing up. Growing entails evolving. We are not instant beings. We have to "become." Hear the Scriptures: "Verily I say unto you, Except ye be converted, and become as little children, ye shall not enter into the Kingdom of Heaven" (Matt. 18:3). "And Jesus said unto them, Come ye after Me, and I will make you to become fishers of men" (Mark 1:17). "But as many as received Him, to them gave He power to become the sons of God, even to them that believe on His Name" (John 1:12). Paul adds: "When I was a child, I spake as a child, I understood as a child, I thought as a child: but when I became a man, I put away childish things" (1 Corin. 13:11).

"Becoming" is the idealisms, the images, the impressions, the individuals, the influences, and the institutions that incorporate our identity. I admit that I am a conglomerate creature. Many people have poured into my life. Many attributes have been emulated and many traits developed. Many performances have been mimicked. It has taken all of these exposures, encounters, environments, engagements, and experiences to establish and to erect me. The combination of the contributing components has been carefully combined to create my choice character. When one is clear, content, and confident in his or her identity, one does not have to be intimidated, inferior, or insecure with any individual.

To perform our tasks in the body or to play our roles in the ministry, it is important that we develop, define, and distinguish ourselves as

Christians. Lack of identity is what causes us to compare, to compete, and to conform our calling to others. This makes service a struggle because we are not shaped like others. When we try to minister with this mind-set, we will lose the ministry God has given us, and we can never succeed at the ministry God has given to someone else. Rick Warren suggests two reasons why we should avoid these actions and these attitudes. "First, you will always be able to find someone who seems to be doing a better job than you and you will become discouraged. Or you will always be able to find someone who doesn't seem as effective as you and you will get full of pride. Either attitude will take you out of service and rob you of your joy."[4]

With a country club membership, one pays others to do the work while one enjoys the "good life." With Church membership, everyone has work to do, a role to play, and a function to fulfill. Many people can remain on the rolls of Churches and never show up or contribute financially to its God-ordained ministry. One can remain an "active member" in some Churches by being CEO Christians: Christmas and Easter Only. One can even be a revered member in a number of Churches by giving a nice sum to the Church each year, even though one never lifts a finger in service or participates in its functions or ministry.

This type of membership is *not* biblical membership. This approach to membership is man-made, man-centered, and man-maintained, and it is wholly contrary to what the Bible teaches. It has no place within the Church of the Lord Jesus Christ. Biblical Church membership serves and ministers as a natural feature of biblical community. Thom S. Rainer writes, "Church membership is more than getting your name on a roll. It's different from the perks and privileges you have when you are in a social club. To the contrary, Church membership is about sacrificing, giving, and forgiving."[5]

The story is told of a man who watched three ants transporting a

---

4. Warren, *Purpose Driven,* 253–254.
5. Thom S. Rainer, *I Am A Church Member: Discovering the Attitude that Makes the Difference* (Nashville, TN: B & H Publishing Group, 2013), 5–6, 10–12, 15, 29.

lump of sugar up Ant Hill. As he watched, he was awestruck when, upon closer observation, he noticed two ants under the load, but the third ant was propped on top of the lump of sugar—simply going along for the ride. The two ants beneath the lump of sugar, within the man's view, were struggling—knees buckling as they bore the weight beneath the load. The third ant, who would benefit in the same way as the others from the lump of sugar once it arrived at Ant Hill, contributed to the weight but not to the work. When the lump of sugar arrived at Ant Hill, the two ants beneath the load would be weary and worn, while the third ant would appear fresh, and most likely eager to share in the newfound bounty.

Sadly, this is a fitting example of the "eighty/twenty concept." Eighty percent of the Church members support and sacrifice, while 20 percent simply sit and spectate. Twenty percent give their monies, generate ministries, and gather for missions, while 80 percent gratify the minimum. If every saint would submit, sacrifice, and share in service, there would be no strain, no struggle, and no stress in service. In fact, everyone's performance would be more pleasant, productive, progressive, and profitable.

Thesis Statement

The Church has been gifted by the Lord with many vital ministries that are available for the growth of the body of Christ. Sadly, the greater percentage of members is neither enrolled nor engaged in the work of the ministry. As a result, a very few members keep the local Church functioning, while the majority of the members (because of what I call *functional paralysis*) has neither the feeling nor the desire to function. Too many congregants are *a part* of the membership but *apart* from the ministry. Too many are unaware or uncaring concerning the needs of the body and of the body's genuine need for them in order to effectively function.

What I describe as "paralysis in the pew" is a grave yet growing spiritual condition within the local Churches. As a physical impediment, paralysis has been drastically improved, even cured, with the aid of physical therapy, prescribed treatments, and personal trust and initiative. It is my contention that parallel treatments—when viewed spiritually and applied in the spiritual and physical realms—can drastically improve, even cure, paralysis in the pew. In order to treat this local Church condition, the paralytic will be prescribed the "three Ds"—develop, discover, and discharge.

1. Develop an intimate relationship within the local Church body

When people unite with a local Church, there is generally an underlying desire to belong to a Church body. They want to fit into a family. They want to be a part of a caring people. They want to be joined together with God's people. For many, being simply a name on the role or a number in the report will not suffice. They need to feel needed in this relationship. They need to feel they can contribute to a genuine need within the community and be recognized for their contributions. To help provide for and promote this process, the Church must work to acclimate, accommodate, and arrange members in these crucial Church relationships. Initially, they will be given a prayer partner, a deacon, a Church-school class and teacher, and a ministry (inclusive of the ministry president). When these individuals have had the opportunity to get to know and to identify with one another, to interact with one another, and to both invest in and be invested in by one another, the likelihood of developing an infinite, individual, and intimate relationship with the body will be greatly enhanced.

2. Discover individual roles in the local Church body

Every piece is needed for the puzzle to be complete. Every part must perform for the automobile to operate correctly. Every organ must function in order for the body to remain healthy. So, too, every member of the local Church is needed for the body to fully produce. The modern Church appears to be the only institution where people desire to become members, occupy a place within the organization, and yet do little (if anything) to help in the overall operation and function of that organization. After being in the Church for years, many members confess, they are still seeking God's will for their lives and searching for the right ministry in which to serve. This does not take place in people's careers. No employee, after having been with a company for any number of years, would say to their employer, "I am trying to find my place in the company." In reality, if a place had not been found within a reasonable length of time, the employee would probably be looking for another job. Yet, this statement is made regularly by members of the local Church.

Members must be made aware of the fact that each believer has a specific calling from God on his or her life and a specific function to fulfill within the Church body. Paul wrote, "But now hath God set the members every one of them in the body, as it hath pleased Him" (1 Corin. 12:18). The preached messages, the prepared material, the provided ministries, and the personal meetings—each can help members find, fill, fit, and fulfill their God-given ministries. Each can help members identify their areas of strength and weakness—their areas of comfort, confidence, contentment, and celebration. In so doing, they can discover the importance of their roles in the body of Christ.

3. Discharge individual responsibility in the local Church body

Once a member has adequately developed relationships with and within the local Church body and discovered and developed a ministry—that is, a role in the local Church—and embraced the importance of that role, he or she can be (and should be) discharged, with adequate oversight and leadership review, to perform his or her individual responsibilities. Many members feel that their contributions will make little difference or that their roles are not really necessary or needed. It is the responsibility of leaders to convey to these individuals the vision—the big picture—and how and where they fit into it. Church leaders must impress upon each member how important each and every ministry is and emphasize the importance of the member's particular role in the realization of the overall vision. When he or she is convinced and convicted that he or she is noticed and genuinely needed, individual responsibilities will be discharged more willingly and joyfully in the local Church. The result will be a healthy, holistic, and harmonious body.

Definition of Terms

For the sake of this project, I felt it best to provide narrative definitions of terms rather than the more routine and somewhat static "dictionary" definitions. In this way, the action, reaction, and interaction of the primary terms used to describe the conditions of the focus groups can be better examined and categorized.

Paralysis

> *Palsy* is a type of *paralysis*. "Paralysis is loss of muscle function for one or more muscles. Paralysis can be accompanied by a loss of feeling (sensory loss) in the affected area if there is sensory damage as well as motor. About one in fifty people have been diagnosed with some form of paralysis, transient or permanent. The word comes from the Greek word παράλυσις, and means a 'disabling of the nerves.' The word itself comes from the two Greek words, παρά (*para*), meaning 'beside or by' and λύσις (*lysis*), meaning 'loosing.' Also from the primary word λύω (*luō*), 'to loose.'"[6]
>
> Paralysis is the inability to move, to maneuver, or to manage the members of the body. For the sake of this study, the definition of *palsy* signifies the body's lack of response to the

6. Henry George Liddell and Robert Scott, "παράλυσις" *A Greek-English Lexicon*. (Oxford: Clarendon Press on Perseus, 1940).

head. Whenever the body rebels, rejects, or refuses the requests of the head, this condition can be called palsy.

Now, Christ is the head of the universal Church. Whenever the body rebels, rejects, or refuses the requests of the head, it is called palsy. Many Churches are suffering with palsy. He has given us our mission (Luke 14:21–23), our ministry (Matt. 25:35–36), and our message (Mark 16:15). And when we do not do it, it is palsy.

Now, the pastor is the visible, physical head of the local Church. And as such, whenever the body rebels, rejects, or refuses the requests of the head, as he or she is under the instruction of the universal head, that too can be called palsy. Many Church members suffering with palsy readily confess their condition. They profess publicly, “I don’t care what the pastor says, I am not going to do it.” The strange thing about it is that they know that the pastor is telling them what is right and what the Word is conveying. We know the Bible commands us to love, to tithe, to forgive, to study, and to pray. But when the pastor puts it before them, they choose not to do it. That can only be called palsy. Whenever the body rebels, rejects, or refuses the requests of the head, this condition is palsy.

Pew

The *pew* is that conglomeration of members within a local Church who, for whatever reason, have consciously or unconsciously made the decision to be “sitters” rather than “servers” and are therefore not actively engaged in ministry.

The pew represents members of the local Church who are not on staff or salaried. Some members are present and participate because they hold positions and are paid. This study is focused on the members who do not hold positions and do not receive a paycheck. The goal is to get these gifted, talented, and skilled members of the Church to become interested, involved, and invested members of the Church.

The Church

The organization and the organism that should operate at its optimum is the Church. There is an idiom we use for ultimate performance: "firing on all cylinders." The expression describes an internal combustion engine with all of its cylinders working and thus providing the maximum amount of power. It is based on a car engine's using all of its cylinders, which are the parts that produce power. "Firing on all cylinders" means working at full strength, making every possible effort.

When each member of the Church is working at maximum power, doing his or her part of the work, and fulfilling his or her role in the body, the Church is firing on all cylinders. When some of the members are slack, slothful, and shirking in service, the Church is "not hitting on all cylinders." When a vehicle is not hitting on all cylinders, the journey is jarring, jerking, and jolting. When a member is not hitting on all cylinders, the ministry strains, struggles, and suffers.

The result of not hitting on all cylinders is paralysis in the pew. Paralysis is the condition that cripples, confines, and complicates the mobility of the ministry. Our focus is to get these members fixed, firing, and functioning. In order for the cylinders of an automobile to hit properly, they must be placed and positioned with precision and care. The term *fixed* implies that members must be set, situated, and stabilized in service. One of the problems in ministry is that most members do not know their place or, as many express, "I have not found God's will for my life." *If members do not know* where they belong in the body, how can they function properly?

I believe this scenario is unique to the body of Christ. If a people were part of an organization or employees of a corporation for over a year, they would know their place, their position, and their requirement of performance. If employees were to ask their employers, after years on the job, "Where am I supposed to be?" and "What am I supposed to be doing?" they would no doubt be dismissed. The Church is the only organization that allows its membership to belong—to be active—without knowing their places in the body or their roles in ministry. The focus of the Church should be getting members "fixed."

Firing on all Cylinders

The focus of the Church should also be on getting its members "fired" (or *fired up*). After members are "fixed," they should be "fired." The term *fired*, in the context of this study, means to get the members excited, energized, and encouraged in the ministry. Nehemiah declared, "for the joy of the LORD is your strength" (Neh. 8:10). Joy is what keeps people going. When there is no joy, labor becomes strenuous and stressful—difficult to remain with companions, difficult to serve in Church, or difficult to support a cause. Our worship, our work, and our walk should have wings, not weights. There should be joy on this journey and on this job. The focus of the Church should be getting members "fired."

Functioning

Finally, the focus of the Church should be getting members functioning. When members are situated and spirited, they want to start serving. Ministry is centered on people. People are responsible for doing ministry, and people are the recipients of ministry. So, without people, there is no ministry. Without people, we can do no ministry. Therefore, the focus of the Church should be getting members functioning.

Minister and Servant

Another term that tends to contribute to paralysis is *minister.* When members hear the word *minister*, their perception is that of one who conducts a religious service, performs a rite, officiates over ceremonies, holds an ecclesiastical office, and administers the ordinances of the Church. The term *minister* as a verb means "to attend to the needs of." A minister is one who ministers. In other words, ministering is meeting a need. My aspiration is that every member becomes a minister because God has placed a ministry in each one of His children.

In my mind, *minister* and *servant* are synonymous. Servanthood is not an area to which one naturally gravitates or aspires. It is not a prestigious position. It is not desired work. In fact, most people think of service as rather degrading—lowly labor or subordinate service.

I reminiscence that as a boy, I sat on the curb of the street among my playmates, hearing different responses to the question, "What do you want to be when you grow up?" The responses varied but included, "doctor," "nurse," "judge," "lawyer," "president," "movie star," "sports star," and other specialties that were the symbols of success. Never once did I hear, "I want to be a servant." And although "a servant" is not often the choice for members of society, it is the calling for saints. The New Testament writers often introduced themselves as servants. Paul introduced himself as a servant in Romans 1:1, Philippians 1:1, and Titus 1:1. Likewise, James introduced himself as a servant (James 1:1), and Peter did the same (2 Peter 1:1). Jude followed suit (Jude 1), and Christ himself was recognized as having come as "a Servant" (Matt. 10:45; Phil. 2:6–7). Each of these individuals helped inspire my very identity. Therefore, *servant* is the label for my labors, the model for my ministry, and the title for my task. *Servant* is on my sign. *Servant* is on my study. And, most importantly, *servant* is in my spirit.

It should go without saying that I have been not only challenged but also criticized and cautioned because of this caption. Pastors, as well as other people, have said to me, "People will have more respect for you and will do more for you if you go by the title 'pastor,' 'overseer,' or some name that elevates you above the people." My response to these comments was that people will have more respect for me as I earn it; respect has to be earned. What earns respect is work, effort, and performance. What earns respect is the way one works, how well one works, and the worth of one's work. One's work builds one's reputation, one's reputation builds one's referrals, and one's referrals build one's respect.

It is my desire to be respected for the work I perform. I want to be respected for my caring for the members, my concern for the missing, my comfort toward the mourning, the chasms I mends, my counseling of the masses, my commitment to the ministry, the contents of my messages, the congregation that is maturing, his conducting of meetings, the choices he makes, the challenges that are met, and the customs that are maintained.

My response to the comment, "people will do more for you …" was, "I cannot reap or receive before I render. I cannot expect to get before I have given. Is this not the way of the earth? Investments come before returns. Sowing comes before reaping. Planting comes before harvest. Testing comes before results. Work comes before wages."

As a leader, my primary concern is not to draw a check but to develop a congregation. My primary concern is not to pad my pockets but to prepare a people. If shepherds feed their sheep, they will get wool. If farmers graze their cows, they will get milk and butter. If gardeners cultivate the ground, they will get crops. If leaders are obedient to the Master in their oversight of the membership, their needs, as well as their obligations, will be met. So, despite the overtones, a servant occupation is my obsession as well as my heartfelt obligation. A servant attitude was what Paul had when he declared, "Yet have I made myself *servant* unto all" (1 Corin. 9:19). I ask your indulgence as I relate this responsibility with that of the waitstaff at a restaurant. In this setting, "a servant" is all of the following:

1. **Assigned a section.** I see the Church as my section. "Take heed therefore unto yourselves, and to all the flock, over the which the Holy Ghost hath made you overseers, to feed the church of God, which He hath purchased with His own blood" (Acts 20:28).
2. **Attentive in service.** As a servant, I am "taking the oversight" (1 Peter 5:2). Paul adds, "Watch thou in all things" (2 Tim. 4:5).
3. **Accommodating in spirit.** The writer of Hebrews suggests that the servant ought to "do it with joy, and not with grief" (Heb. 13:17). David adds, "Serve the Lord with gladness" (Ps. 100:2).
4. **Available when summoned.** "And I heard the voice of the Lord, saying, Whom shall I send, and who will go for us? Then said I, Here am I; send me" (Is. 6:8).
5. **Aspiring to satisfy.** "Even as I please all men in all things, not seeking my own profit, but the profit of many, that they may be saved" (1 Corin. 10:33). Jesus said, "For I do always those things that please Him" (John 8:29).

Jonathan Leeman moves us from the act of service to the attitude of the servant. He suggests that the Church member is called to submission. In his book titled *Church Membership,* he describes eight ways to submit.

1. **Publicly**. "Jesus publicly identified Himself with His Church. We should publicly identify with Him and His people as well—by joining a Church."[7] I believe we publicly submit to Christ and to the Church through affiliation. When we stand and confess before the congregation, "I want to be a part" and "I want to belong to

7. Jonathan Leeman, *Church Membership: How the World Knows Who Represents Jesus* (Wheaton, IL: Crossway Publishing, 2012), 95.

the body," we publicly submit to Christ and to the Church through attendance. The Church is competing with celebrations, clubs, concerts, and casinos for the crowd. Most times, the secular events win over the sacred events. The submission is when we prefer assembling with the saints over and against other attractions and other activities. The writer of the Hebrews wrote, "Not forsaking the assembling of ourselves together, as the manner of some is; but exhorting one another: and so much the more, as ye see the day approaching" (Heb. 10:25).

2. **Physically**. "Christians should submit to their local Churches physically and perhaps geographically. We submit physically by gathering regularly with the Church (Heb. 10:25; Acts 2:42–47)."[8] I place emphasis on the physical. Many members say, "I am with you in spirit" or "I am sending my spirit." The Church does not need you to send your spirit. The Church has the Holy Spirit. The Church is the one place, if not the only place, we send our spirit. Ironically, we do not send our spirit to the grocery store or to the bank or on an excursion. The Church needs you physically. We cannot fellowship with, study with, and pray with your spirit. We should submit to Christ and to the Church physically. Luke records of the early Church, "And they continued steadfastly in the apostles' doctrine and fellowship, and in breaking of bread, and in prayers" (Acts 2:42).
3. **Socially**. "The local Church community should be a place where Christians form and shape one another for good through all the dynamics of friendship. Christian friends are surely valuable inside or outside the same local Church."[9] The author believes relationships are important in the local Church. The Church should guard against becoming a social place where saints gather to catch up on the latest occurrences. Church should be a place where people of like beliefs can come together and

---

8. Leeman, *Church Membership*, 96.
9. Leeman, *Church Membership*, 98.

build relationships and rapport within its ranks that will be real, resourceful, and reassuring. Saints should share and support one another between Sundays.

4. **Affectionately.** "Christians should submit their affections to one another (1 Corin. 12:25b–26; Rom. 12:10), fulfilling Paul's command to 'value others better than yourselves' with 'the same love,' knowing the love of Him Who did not consider equality with God something to be grasped, and then loving like Him."[10] Is this not what Jesus commended and commanded? "A new commandment I give unto you, That ye love one another; as I have loved you, that ye also love one another. By this shall all men know that ye are My disciples, if ye have love one to another" (John 13:34–35). We should be attentive to and active in the needs of the saints. Paul wrote to the Church at Galatia, "As we have therefore opportunity, let us do good unto all men, especially unto them who are of the household of faith" (Gal. 6:10). Many join Churches expecting others to serve them and to care for them. "God placed us in Church to serve, to care for others, to pray for leaders, to learn, to reach, to give, and, in some cases, to die for the sake of the Gospel."[11] As we mature in Christ, the focus of our lives should increasingly shift to living a life of service. The mature follower of Jesus stops asking, "Who's going to meet my needs?" and starts asking, "Whose needs can I meet?"[12]
5. **Financially.** "Christians should submit themselves to their local Churches financially" (Rom. 12:13; 1 Corin. 16:1–2; Gal. 6:6).[13] Money is a tough and touchy topic in the Church. There are few subjects on which the Lord's own people are more astray than on the subject of giving. They profess to take the Bible

---

10. Leeman, *Church Membership*, 98–99.
11. Rainer, *I Am a Church Member*, 6.
12. Warren, *Purpose Driven Life*, 231.
13. Leeman, *Church Membership*, 99.

as their only rule of faith and practice, and yet in the matter of Christian finance, the vast majority have utterly ignored its plain teachings and have tried every substitute the carnal mind could devise; therefore, it is no wonder that the majority of Christian enterprises in the world today are handicapped and crippled through the lack of funds.

God is interested in our money because money is the supreme test of where our hearts are. Jesus said, "For where your treasure is, there will your heart be also" (Matt. 6:21). So if God can get us to invest our money with him and in him, he knows that our hearts will soon show up. He issued the decree to Israel, "Bring ye all the tithes." It stands to reason that members of the Church want the best for their Church, and having the best requires giving. It takes more than faith to function; it takes finances to function. It takes more than motive to minister; it takes money to minister. We must remove the myth that the Church can function without funds. That is why God established the financial plan for the Church, which is tithes and offering (Mal. 3:8–10).

6. **Vocationally**. "Christians should submit their vocations to their Church. For some people, this means going into vocational ministry. By the way, some of the best non-staff elders in a Church are not the men who move up the professional ladder but the men who are willing to move down it for the sake of the Church."[14] On the hills of tithes, I recommend tithing your vocation. There are many professionals in the membership of the Church who can help defray Church expense by donating their experience and their expertise to the Church. Many will and do jobs in lieu of donations. Jesus said, *"It is more blessed to give than to receive"* (Acts 20:35).

---

14. Leeman, *Church Membership*, 100–101.

7. **Ethically.** "Christians should look to the Church for ethical instruction, counsel, accountability, and discipline in matters that are addressed by God's Word."[15] It is my conviction that the Church should dispense the doctrine, the decorum, the directions, the discipline, and the duties for disciples. The psalmist declares, "For the Word of the LORD is right; and all His works are done in truth" (Ps. 33:4).
8. **Spiritually**. Paul wrote, "If we live in the Spirit, let us also walk in the Spirit" (Gal. 5:25). Our words, our works, and our worship should be spiritual. The problem stated and defined is the inability of our ability. God has endowed, entrusted, and empowered each believer to do ministry. Every believer is able to do all God has asked, assigned, and appointed him or her to do. The problem is inability. I credit the inability to the insecurity, the inferiority, and the intimidation of individuals to be involved and to be instruments in ministry.

---

15. Leeman, *Church Membership*, 101.

Chapter 2

BIBLICAL AND THEOLOGICAL STUDY OF THE PROBLEM

The Bible addresses, answers, and has the antidote for every ailment in the anatomy of the Christian assembly. Nothing surprises the Lord. As Solomon so rightly surmises in Ecclesiastes 1:9, "There is nothing new under the sun." The following Scriptures and theological deductions not only reinforce Solomon's conclusion but also show that God's Word is relevant for the modern-day problem focus of this study. God has the answer: "For I know the thoughts that I think toward you, saith the LORD, thoughts of peace, and not of evil, to give you an expected end" (Jer. 29:11).

I believe that, before our entrance into this world, before we knew we were posing, God took a picture of each of us. He took the negatives of that picture into the darkroom of his divinity, placed those negatives in the chemical solution of his celestial spectrum, and set the timer of truth until the perfect portrait was exposed in eternity. That portrait is on display in the gallery of glory and is God's plan for each life.

The portrait is detailed with our purpose, our path, our pursuits, and our place. God said, "'For I know the plans I have for you,' declares the LORD, 'plans to prosper you and not to harm you, plans to give you hope and a future'" (Jer. 29:11 NIV).[16] The Message Bible translates the verse: "I know what I'm doing. I have it all planned out—plans to take care of you, not abandon you, plans to give you the future you hope for" (Jer. 29:11 MSG).[17] God prepares us for our purpose. In Jeremiah 1:5, God said to Jeremiah, "Before I formed thee in the belly I knew thee; and before thou camest forth out of the womb I sanctified thee, and I ordained thee a prophet unto the nations." This is the verse that convicted, compelled, and confirmed my call. This is my *personal* interpretation of this very telling verse. The word *knew* is a very forceful Hebrew word reflecting intimacy. To "know" someone is to have "a personal awareness" and a "purposeful affection." Birth is not man's beginning, nor is conception his true genesis. In some deep, divine way, God has a personal, intimate knowledge of the individual that precedes conception. "Before I formed thee in the belly I knew thee."

So when did Jeremiah start belonging to God? When did God choose him? The Scriptures announce that the prophet was set apart before he was born. Before conception, God was making preparations for his salvation and for his service. God said, "I sanctified thee." God set him apart, dedicated him to holy service. Long before Jeremiah was born, God chose him and consecrated him for his calling and his work. Not only did God "know" Jeremiah "before," but I believe Jeremiah "knew" God "before." Eugene Peterson offers the following conclusion:

> Our identity does not begin when we begin to understand ourselves. We entered the world in which the essential parts of our existence were already ancient history. There is something previous to what we think about ourselves, and it is what God thinks of us. That means that everything we think and feel is by nature a response, and the One to whom we respond is God.[18]

---

16. *New International Version Bible* (Grand Rapids, MI: Zondervan, 2014).
17. *The Message Bible* (Carol Stream, IL: NavPress. 2010).
18. Eugene H. Peterson, *Run with the Horses: The Quest for Life at Its Best* (Downers Grove, IL: InterVarsity Press, 1983), 38.

I believe that God prepares our agenda before our arrival. Our lives should fulfill the calling God has placed on our lives. We should seek to please Him in the purpose, the path, the pursuit, and the place He planned for us. We are guilty of straying from God's path for our labor and from His plan for our life. If we are to please God, our concentration and our commitment must be to His calling and to His choice.

In 2009, Julian Jones directed a movie entitled *The Great Sperm Race.* Scientific study revealed there are 250 million sperm cells released during sexual intercourse. With 250 million competitors, it is the most extreme race on earth—and birth will be granted, in most cases, only to one. Therefore, conception is the grace of God. He allowed us to enter this world to seek him, to serve him, and to satisfy him.

> For by grace are ye saved through faith; and that not of yourselves: it is the gift of God: Not of works, lest any man should boast. For we are his workmanship, created in Christ Jesus unto good works, which God hath before ordained that we should walk in them. (Eph. 2:8–10)

Seldom do individuals truly hear verse 10 in this passage. They read verses 8 and 9 for the pellucidity of their salvation. They stop at verse 9 and never reach verse 10, which gives the purpose of this salvation: that they are saved to serve. Saul understood this when he faced Christ on the Damascus Road. He came, all too starkly, to understand that he was pulled over for a purpose. He asked, "Lord, what wilt Thou have me to do?" (Acts 9:6). Christ did not save us for the showcase, as a souvenir, or for the trophy shelf. He saved us to serve. Saul understood this.

> Then the word of the LORD came to me, saying, O house of Israel, cannot I do with you as this potter? saith the LORD. Behold, as the clay is in the potter's hand, so are ye in mine hand, O house of Israel. (Jer. 18:5–6)

God sent Jeremiah to the potter's house. It can be presumed that the potter's house had two sides. When Jeremiah was sent there, he was sent to the shop, not the showroom, which would be for the clay vessels that had been completed. The shop, however, was for the clay that was yet under construction. Potters have creative minds. Potters design the clay for human service just as God designs the Christian for divine service. Potters decide what they want the clay to be based upon their appetites, their assignments, and their needs. They know what they want or need in their service. The ideas and the images are in the minds of the potters. The potters determine what they want to develop. They decide if the piece is to be a kettle, a pot, a bottle, a vase, a cup, a plate, a saucer, or a bowl. They know what they want. They know the plans they have for the clay.

When human potters decide what the clay is to become, the clay does not have a say in the decision (see Isaiah 45:9). The clay cannot suggest its shape, size, or service. The clay remains submissive to, and must be satisfied with, the potter's plan and purpose.

Likewise, Christians do not choose their gifts, their talents, their abilities, or their skills. God determines those. He knows what He wants from each person. In addition, each product has its own distinction. No product is designed to do what another product is designed to do. Author Rick Warren brings this point forward.

> Only you can be you. God designed each of us so there would be no duplication in the world. No one has the exact same mix of factors that make you unique. That means no one else on earth will ever be able to play the role God planned for you. If you don't make your unique contribution to the Body of Christ, it won't be made.[19]

---

19. Warren, *The Purpose Driven Life*, 241.

Likewise, the Scriptures disclose this truth. "But now hath God set the members every one of them in the body, as it hath pleased Him" (1 Cor. 12:18).

In 1 Corinthians 12, Paul uses the metaphor of the body to explain Church membership. Paul points out that each member is set in the body to serve, to support, and to strengthen the body. No one member is the whole body. No one member can do or be everything. In order for the body to function properly, however, each member must do his or her part.

The author understands through Scripture that when Christ saves people, He "sets" them. To *set* implies a place—there is a place for them. They do not choose the place; Christ does. For this reason, Christians must be both prayerful and careful to follow the Spirit's leading when seeking a Church home. Some have expressed that they feel out of place in their Church homes. Granted, some feel this way due to various human feelings or extenuating situations. However, if we are not in God's set place—if we are not where God wants us to be—we are, in fact, out of place. When a person is out of place, he or she will not fit and will not fit in.

This understanding is important because *set* also implies permanency. As Christians, we should *not* be flocking from fellowship to fellowship. We should remain firm, faithfully established and contributing in one. Reflect back upon the day when people were identified with Churches because of longevity. Today it is difficult to associate individuals with particular Churches because they change membership or attendance so frequently. People are set by God so that they can be established and become effective in the ministry to which they have been gifted and called.

Set implies a purpose for each and every person. Every part of the body has a function. Each function is necessary for the working of the whole. Likewise, there is a function for every member of the body of Christ. "Members are not given permission to 'warm a pew' and do nothing else, for God places each member in the Church for a reason. Paul simply would not have understood the phrase 'uninvolved Church member.'"[20]

The fact is that others need what each person has. God has a unique role for each member in His family to play. This is called ministry, and God has gifted each for an assignment. The local fellowship is the place God designed within which each member discovers, develops, and uses his or her gifts. Some may have wider ministries, but that is in addition to their service in a local body. The Church must understand that there is no life or labor from any one member of the body that is not connected in some way to the whole. If an organ is severed from its body, it will shrivel and die. It cannot exist on its own, and neither can the individual member of the body of Christ. Disconnected—cut off from the lifeblood of a body—the individual will spiritually wither and eventually cease to function. In Ephesians 4:16, Paul writes, "From whom the whole body fitly joined together and compacted by that which every joint supplieth, according to the effectual working in the measure of every part, maketh increase of the body unto the edifying of itself in love."

The gospel artist Hezekiah Walker composed a song titled "I Need You to Survive." His lyrics include the following encouragement: "I need you, you need me. We're all a part of God's body. Stand with me, agree with me. We're all a part of God's body."

Set implies partnership. We are not set to ourselves, nor are we set by ourselves. We are to be with and among others. There is no such thing as a lone ranger Christian. Some Christians try to work individually and independently of others, as if they do not need anything from anyone else. In 1 Corinthians 12:21, the statement "I have no need of you" occurs twice. The perception is that some members do not really need other members to accomplish their designated ministries. By implication, this is because they feel that they are so individually capable—so highly

---

[20] Chuck Lawless and Thom S. Rainer, *Membership Matters: Insights from Effective Churches on New Member Classes and Assimilation* (Grand Rapids, MI: Zondervan. 2005), 73.

qualified. This can only be viewed as pride, possessing an independent spirit and an attitude of autonomy. Each of these ideas is not only untrue but completely unacceptable before God.

It is alarming that in so many congregations people embrace the idea that they do not need the rest of the body; that they can function on their own; that they have their own distinct abilities and unique ministries; and that they can do things quite well apart from others in the body of Christ. This will always engender a sense of exclusivity, a rise in unwarranted competitiveness, or a spirit of rivalry. None are acceptable before the Father.

Likewise, it is sadly common for people who have been gifted with what might be classified as more prominent abilities to become self-sufficient and, in too many cases, even selective about the people with whom they will surround themselves. They are quite selective about the friendships they develop and too easily can become a lone ranger in ministry. It becomes too easy, if gifted in a significant way, to overestimate one's own importance or worth and to undervalue the contribution of other believers.

Notice, however, how the apostle puts it: "parts we think less honorable." In all reality, they are not less honorable at all. It is simply one's idea of them that makes them appear that way. We can carefully take mental account of this perception and try to work it to our advantage. I believe Paul is referring to what are often called the "private" parts or the "unpresentable parts." However, in all realty, we do treat these parts with a greater modesty. Paul simply draws the analogy with the body of Christ. He says there are hidden, secret functions within the body, never mentioned in public, that are nevertheless exceedingly important.

A doctor, in conversation with a preacher, said, "You may be interested to know that there is a certain part of your body that is absolutely essential to you as a preacher. You probably do not even think about it when you are preaching, and yet without it you could not do the work you are doing. Do you know what it is?" The preacher said, "No. Is it my tongue, or my brain?" "No," the doctor said. "Those are obvious. It's your big toe. Did you know that if you didn't have a big toe on each foot, you could not even stand up to preach? It is the toe that has the ability to sense when your body begins to lean, or shift, or get out of balance, or fall, and it immediately strengthens you so that you can stand up and speak." So now we understand—we have to guard each big toe because we need it! It is an essential part of ministry.

Set implies prominence. No one is an insignificant member of the body. Each is an important, necessary member of the body of Christ. Status is not determined by size. If one is a member of the body, he or she has a prominent position. Twice in 1 Corinthians 12:15–16, we see the words, "I am not a part of the body." The perception that the body does not really need them or that they have nothing to contribute to the body represents the temptation to believe that they really have no gifts or abilities that are valuable or worthwhile. The temptation is to sit back and let others do the work of ministry. The attitude of the foot and the ear may reflect the feeling of some people in the body. Individuals may feel that they don't really matter in their Church or that their gifting is inferior, insignificant, or unimportant when compared to that of others.

If viewed carefully, the analogy of the foot and the ear reflects an underlying attitude of jealousy. Looking at it from their perspective, they appear jealous because of the obvious and observable necessity of the hand and the eye. All a foot can do is support the rest of the body when it stands, and then it cooperates with the other necessary members when the body is walking, bending, stooping down, and so on. The foot is rarely allowed to be in public view. Usually (though mainly out of necessity), it is covered up with a sock and shoe, hidden away from public scrutiny. Thinking of the ear, it is often viewed as nothing more than a receptor, waiting for occasional sound waves to arrive. It may be said that it is not a very attractive receptor at that. It is often covered over with hair or a muff or used as a hanger for attractive jewelry in an attempt to make it a bit more attractive than it is normally. No wonder ears may feel inferior!

In this parable, neither the foot nor the ear appears to understand its importance or the contribution it makes individually to the body when used in conjunction with the hand or the eye. The hand has the ability to touch most anything it wants; the ability to pick things up and move them around; and the ability to use tools. However, without the foot to move the body to a place within adequate reach, the hand cannot accomplish the task it is intended or designed to do. The ear may hear danger coming, but without the eye to guide the body, the body's reaction could just as easily lead the body into more danger as lead it away to safety. One could easily make a list of ways the hand, eye, foot, and ear function together, cooperatively, for the health and well-being of the body.

In verse 17, Paul makes the point that contrary thinking is, in reality, quite absurd. If everyone in the Church felt like the lowly foot and ear and could choose to be something else, the body would simply be one huge eye. They would be able to see magnificently! They could see the vast possibilities that lay before them. They could view the grand plan of God before them, but they would not be able to do a single thing about what they saw. Or, if the whole body were one giant ear, they would be able to hear remarkably well! They could hear the cries of the lost and hurting and understand their need clearly. They could hear the voices of the other members of the body of Christ and recognize their needs, but they would not be able to do a single thing about what they heard. The body would be able to hear well, but it would not be able to smell. Paul is parodying those who say, "Because I do not have a certain spiritual gift, I am not really important or an important part of the Church." Others may say, "My gift is second-rate and unnecessary. I have nothing to offer, so why should I participate?"

What is seen is a talking foot or ear who feels jealously inferior to a hand or an eye, and because of that jealousy they threaten to desert the body, leaving it unable to move forward in the Lord's work (to walk) or to discern the Lord's voice and direction (to hear). This passage makes clear the reality that each and every part is needed and that disclaiming, denying, or disdaining that responsibility does not diminish the need or decommission the commission. Drawing back from functioning as part of the body does not make us any less a part of the body. Paul says this twice, at the end of verse 15 and at the end of verse 16. His thesis is this:

there are no inferior or insignificant members of the body of Christ. "Then saith He unto His disciples, The harvest truly is plenteous, but the labourers are few; Pray ye therefore the Lord of the harvest, that He will send forth labourers into His harvest" (Matt. 9:37–38).

The burden of the Church is not that we have nothing to do. We have a mandate, a mission, and a ministry from the Master. But truly, there is not enough manpower. We have more work than workers, more wheat than winnowers. I submit that the Church has the highest of unemployment rates. We have too many believers who are not busy, too many Christians who are not committed, too many individuals who are idle, and too many saints who are sitting. It is harvest time. The field is ripe, and we are shorthanded. In Luke 10:2, Jesus said, "The harvest is plenteous, but the laborers are few."

The gospel of Matthew tells us, "Jesus went" (Matt. 9:35). Jesus went everywhere. The course, concern, and compassion of Christ were not confined. The love, labor, and life of the Lord were not limited. The message, ministry, and mission of the Master were not minimized. He went into all the cities and villages (Matt. 9:35). He went into the synagogues (Matt. 9:35). He went by the seashore (Matt. 4:18). He went onto mountains (Matt. 5:1). He went in boats (Matt. 8:23). He went through graveyards (Matt. 8:28). He went into homes (Matt. 8:14; 9:10). He went. And as He went, He observed.

In His goings, Jesus saw the condition of the people, and it moved Him. It can be surmised that their condition was threefold. First, they were spent; some were faint, and others were fainting. To faint is "to lose heart; to be faint; to be discouraged; to give up; to give out; to lose heart; to collapse; to buckle under; to lose courage; to weaken."[21] In Scripture, the word is used when a person has struggled against sin or stood against attacks—insult after insult—until he or she can no longer stand. It means that a person has undergone trial after trial until he or she is ready to collapse. Second, the people were scattered abroad.

---

21. Donald A. Nash, *Practical New Testament Word Studies* (Christian Restoration Assn., 1982).

When sheep are driven from a fold, they do not run together in a flock. Rather, they scatter over mountains and through valleys, each running its own way. This is what Jesus saw in the multitudes. They were scattered, each going his or her own way. In the cities and villages, He saw men going, every one, after different things. Some were going after money, making it their chief good. They toiled night and day over their work yet did not enjoy the money they made. Some were going after pleasure: the wine, the dance and song, the pipe and the drum. Frivolity was their companion. Others were going after the carnal pleasures of deep carousal, glorying in their debauchery and shame. Third, the people were as sheep without a shepherd. Being without a shepherd or caring guide, they had no firm direction (no pilot to guide them), no nourishing diet (no provider to graze them), and no solid defense (no protector to guard them).

This was a critical time for ministry. If the harvest was not gathered, it would spoil in the field. What was the recourse? Jesus said to pray! "Pray ye therefore the Lord of the harvest, that He will send forth labourers into His harvest" (Matt. 9:38). In this day, the call remains, for the need remains. My deepest desire is that the Church will heed His call and hear His voice again and afresh, that Christians will once again come and commit to changing and to curing the conditions of our world through the healing gospel of Jesus Christ. After all, this is our time.

E. E. Hewitt composed the hymn "Count on Me." This cry that I desire to hear in the Church is reflected in the composer's words. The lyrics, in part, read,

> The Lord has need of workers to till His field today, so kindly He has led me to walk in wisdom's way; I pray for grace to help me with all my heart to say, O blessed Savior, count on me. Count on me, count on me, For loving hearten service glad and free; Yes, count on me, count on me, O blessed Savior, count on me.

In Matthew 25:14–30, Jesus tells the parable of a man traveling to a far country and leaving his business in the hands of three servants. Two servants were faithfully active and doubled their given talents. The third servant, however, was unfaithful and inactive and buried his talent in the earth. This servant said fear was the reason for his inactivity. "Then he which had received the one talent came and said, Lord, I knew thee that thou art an hard man, reaping where thou hast not sown, and gathering where thou hast not strawed: And I was afraid, and went and hid thy talent in the earth: lo, there thou hast that is thine" (Matt. 25:24–25).

The man who received the one talent expressed his excuse for failure—fear! The man said, "I was afraid." In essence the man was saying, 'The reason I did nothing, the reason I did not get involved, was fear." Though there is more to the story than the unfaithful, inactive servant's flimsy excuse, this Scripture touched something in my spirit when I thought about various members in the Church in which I currently serve.

I had been seeking answers to the following questions: "Why are members comfortable with just coming to Church?" "Why are members satisfied with simply sitting in the pew?" "Why are members meeting simply to maintain their membership?" I was seeking an answer to the questions, "Why aren't some Christians contributing to the Church?" "Why aren't some saints serving in His service?" "Why aren't some members ministering for the Master?" "Why aren't some congregants committed to the cause of Christ?"

The conclusion was not that there was inactivity because there was nothing to be done. Jesus said, "The harvest truly is plenteous, but the labourers are few" (Matt. 9:37). If one would simply browse the many ministries included in the vision for the Church, the tremendous need for laborers would be obvious. There are needs all around us. There is much work to be done. There are vacancies to be filled. There is more to do as part of the Church than simply singing and ushering. There are other ministries awaiting and available. One of the biggest reasons that individuals are inactive is intimidation. Fear! In the words of the servant who received the one talent, "I was afraid."

Far too often, the reason for failure is fear. People are fearful of relationships. People are fearful of taking risks. People are fearful of taking on responsibilities because they do not want to fail. Understandably, other elements are present in this very telling parable. However, it is my strong contention that the element of fear—in this case, the fear of failure—is itself the greatest contributing factor in failure itself. While this man was fearful of failing, it was his fear that caused him to fail.

In the parable about the man traveling to a far country who left his goods with his three servants, these goods had value. They were particularly valuable to the man who had left them. These goods can be representative of talents, treasures, or things. They could include those precious elements of time, personal ties (family, friends, and fellowships), and things. The man did not close the business or relocate it because he was going into the far country. He left the business in the charge of these three servants. When Jesus took His journey back to the Father, He did not take the Kingdom business with Him or relocate it to heaven. Jesus left the "business" here upon the earth. He left His business in the hands of His servants, the Church.

Let us return focus to the man with the one talent. "He that had received one went and digged in the earth, and hid his lord's money" (Matt. 25:18). Attention is called to what the man buried: "his lord's money." He buried that which had been given him. Though it may seem insignificant or appear rather trite on the surface, that "one" represented precious possibilities to the lord who had entrusted it to him. If viewed from a broader perspective, it represented the following:

- Position—The "goods" advanced him from servant to supervisor, from a common laborer to a chosen leader.
- Property—He had nothing of himself or of his own. He was now a trusted steward.
- Potential—The "one" had great potential. Look what "one" accomplished: the one pot of oil (2 Kings 4:1–7); one boy's lunch (John 6:9–15); the only son on Calvary.

A commercial on television spoke about the power of "one voice." And remember, every journey begins with one step! The power and potential of one is far greater than some may fully understand.

I previously stated that Christians can often fear relationships, risks, and responsibilities. The fact that the man with the one talent buried his gift suggests a number of possibilities.

1. No commitment to relationship. The servant should have done business with his one talent. The size of the responsibility did not matter to the lord. If he possessed even the slightest devotion or loyalty to his master, he should have done *something*. His refusal to serve reveals a lack of love and little desire to accomplish anything for the master. Jesus said, "And why call ye Me, Lord, Lord, and do not the things which I say?" (Luke 6:46).

2. No courage to risk. Anyone who attempts to do something for God will experience some degree of fear of failure—some more than others. However, he will never please the Lord or succeed in his work unless he is willing to risk. We have not been called to comfort. We will be given times of rest by the Lord, but a life of leisure is not our calling. Sometimes, coming to Christ or being called to serve Him means we have to step out of our comfort zones. It may mean that we have to do something that we would not normally envision ourselves doing. It may mean expending some effort, some energy, or even some expense to accomplish God's will. It may also mean laying aside our will in order to do the will of the Father.

It was not a comfortable thing for Peter to leave his nets (and therefore, his livelihood) to follow after Jesus. It was not a comfortable thing for Moses to obey God's call and lead the people of Israel out of bondage and into the promised land—even at great emotional and physical cost. God has called us as well. God has called us to use our gifts, out talents, and our time in His service and for His Kingdom. This may not always be comfortable; sometimes, we will discover that we are quite comfortable when we are and where we are able to use our gifts and talents. Far too many people will never use their gifts to the fullest simply because they are much too comfortable where they currently are—they want no new challenges. They have things "under control," wanting only the same comfortable place.

But in all honesty, we take risks each and every day. We take a risk when we get in our cars and drive. We take a risk when we dine out and try a new restaurant. We take a risk when we enter our workplace and the boss gives us a new job. We take a risk when we make a bank deposit, trusting the employees to be honest. We take a risk when we tell others our business, hoping we will not be ridiculed. We take risk every day. Yet, when it comes to taking a risk for God—taking a risk in ministry, using our skills or testing our abilities, exercising our gifts, and trusting God for the outcome—we are afraid.

3. No conscientiousness of responsibility. One would think that if someone left a person a business to operate or a department to manage, there would be something the person should be doing. This man was neither responsive nor responsible. He was selfish and self-centered. He did not want to be bothered. Before we look too harshly on this man, we must look at ourselves, as well. We too can be extremely selfish. We do not want to give or give up (a) ourselves—temple, (b) our schedule—time, (c) our substance—treasure, or (d) our service—task. Consequently, do we not also bury what God gives us and what God assigns our hands to do?

The parable reminds us that we are accountable for (going to give account of) that which has been assigned to us. When the owner returned and called for a report, the servant with the one talent made excuses instead of recognizing that, from the beginning, his responsibility was to serve his master to the best of his ability. Having buried his gift, he was labeled as wicked (v. 26), wasteful (v. 27), and worthless (v. 30).

Fear of using our gifts often hinders us from being what God has designed us to be. Fear is never an adequate excuse for not using what God has entrusted to our care. In the end, God is concerned about what we do with what we have been given. The question Jesus will ask us is this: What have you done with that which I entrusted to you?

God's people must not let fear of failure entice them to fail. Each one must try. We must put forth the effort to discover, develop, and deliver the talents that have been entrusted to our care for the betterment of the Kingdom of God. God will forgive failure if one tries. However, He will not forgive failure to try. As the hymnodists J. R. Baxter and Lucie E. Campbell penned:

> But if you try and fail in your trying, Hands sore and scarred from the work you've begun; Take up your cross, run quickly to meet Him, He'll understand; He'll say, "Well Done."[22]

Paul's words to Timothy should be our constant encouragement: "For God hath not given us the spirit of fear; but of power, and of love, and of a sound mind" (2 Tim. 1:7).

Jesus also presented His disciples with the parable of the barren fig tree. In it He stressed to the Jews as well as His disciples that God desired "fruit" from His children. The parable is a rather probing passage that was intended to prick the conscience of the hearers and prod them to become producing, profiting practitioners for the Kingdom.

> He spake also this parable; A certain man had a fig tree planted in his vineyard; and he came and sought fruit thereon, and found none. Then said he unto the dresser of his vineyard, Behold, these three years I come seeking fruit on this fig tree, and find none: cut it down; why cumbereth it the ground? And he answering said unto him, Lord, let it alone this year also, till I shall dig about it, and dung it: And if it bear fruit, well: and if not, then after that thou shalt cut it down" (Luke 13:6–9).

The "certain man" in this parable is a businessman, the owner of a vineyard that included fig trees. The purpose of any business is to produce a product that is both profitable and pleasing to the buying

---

22. J. R. Baxter and Lucie E. Campbell, "He'll Understand and Say Well Done," *Lyrics Universal Music Publishing Group*, http://www.metrolyrics.com/hell-understand-and-say-well-done-lyrics-ferlin-husky.html

public. The proprietor undoubtedly wanted the business to be profitable. The way to accomplish this was to plant a healthy, productive, and promising plant. It is understood that this is what the proprietor planned when he planted the fig tree. The owner planted what he wanted. He knew his taste. He knew his desires and his appetite, so he planted what he liked. He anticipated that one day he would have a craving for figs, so he planted a fig tree. Figs were his preference. If he had wanted something else, he would have planted something else. He planted the fig tree in the vineyard so it would be in good soil, in a good growing environment, and receive the best possible care. It was anticipated that, in due season, the fig tree would bear fruit that would be beneficial to his household and profitable to his business. Yet after three years, though the fig tree was sitting on the premises, settled in a prime position, it was not serving its purpose. Likewise, we, as Christians and members of the body of Christ, were planted in the Church (as well as in *a Church*) to be active, producing assets for the advancement of that assembly and the Kingdom. Yet members of our local Churches remain on the Church rolls, come regularly to service, respond, and claim rights but do not carry responsibilities.

To bring this point a bit closer to home, the fig tree (or for the sake of this example, we shall call it "Fig") is idle, inoperative, ineffective, insipid, and indifferent. It is my observation that Fig shows no regret or remorse and intends no repentance for its nonresponsiveness. It does not bother Fig that it is drawing sap and draining strength (nutrients) from the other trees in the vineyard. It does not disturb Fig that the burden to bear the products, beautify the vineyard, or bless the people with bounty was placed upon the other trees. In like manner, inactivity did not seem to impose, inconvenience, irritate, or irk some individuals. These are the members of our Churches who are not bothered by the serving, the sacrificing, and the supporting of others by some while they sit, see, and shirk. There are also members of our Churches who are not disturbed by the tasks others are doing, the time others are devoting, and the tithes others are disbursing while their talents are never displayed. They can stay and sit and be satisfied in not serving (not producing).

"He came" implies that the owner of the vineyard had certain expectations. The owner had a right to expect some fruit from this fig tree. As was mentioned, Fig was in a good area, receiving good attention and assistance. All Fig needed to be productive was provided. With all the time, effort and energy invested in the fig tree, the owner had every right to expect some fruit. Likewise, after all God has done for His children, the Lord has a right to expect fruit from each of His children, as well. After all, He bought us at a cost, He delivered us from the bondage of sin and death, He saved us from the eternal torment of hell, He has filled us with His Holy Spirit, He has loved us, and He died for us. Could anyone deny that He has a right to expect us to bear fruit for Him? And, what kind of fruit is He seeking? He is seeking the fruit of the Spirit, the fruit of our service, and the fruit of our support.

It must be understood that the owner of the fig tree did not expect more from the tree than it could give. Neither did he expect something from the tree anything that was against its nature or design. The only thing the owner wanted from the fig tree was figs. Because this tree produced no figs, it did not fulfill the need or intent of the owner. The fruitlessness of the fig tree was the fault of the tree, not the owner. It appears that the fig tree had been provided with all that it needed to bear fruit. The problem was that it did not respond in a productive way to what the owner had provided. Its efforts were empty. The investment gave no increase. The labor was lost. The work was worthless. In all that was done, no fruit was found.

The owner asked the dresser, "Why cumbereth it the ground?" The owner was questioning why the tree was still taking up space in the vineyard. Why is this tree here when it is not producing anything? Why is it still here? A fig tree is only good for its fruit. If a fig tree is not producing figs, it is good for nothing but firewood. No other part of the tree is useful. You cannot use its leaves for fertilizer. You cannot use its limbs for a walking cane, not even a switch. A fig tree is only good for its fruit.

Finally, we see the vinedresser interceding for Fig: "Let it alone this year also." In other words, *Give me a little more time to work with it,* he pleaded with the owner. *Do not send me to bring the ax. Rather, send me to bring a shovel. Let me dig about it and dung it.* One will notice here that the vinedresser planned to do all the work for the barren fig tree on its roots. The vinedresser knew that anything that was wrong with the tree had to do with its roots. The roots of the tree needed to respond to the work of the vinedresser.

When one looks at the Church and its members and sees that there is life and leaves (in other words, it looks good on the outside) but there is no fruit, it must be remembered that the problem is in the roots. Another way of putting it is that the problem is in the heart. The heart of the problem is a problem of the heart. The Holy Spirit is continually working on our hearts in an attempt to make us fruitful and productive. But we must respond to His work; we must yield to His wooing, hear His voice, and obey.

The vinedresser said, "If it bear fruit, well: and if not, then after that thou shalt cut it down." The full measure of all that cultivating may entail is open to broad speculation. But suffice to say, it could not be good. Causing people to bear fruit is what the Holy Spirit is attempting in our lives. This is his intent. This is His mission in the Church. " … and if not, then after that thou shalt cut it down." Many will want to know what happened to Fig. But what is more important is what will happen to each of us as believers. The outcome of Fig and of each of us depends on our fruit. What has God designed us to be and to produce? Are we bearing our fruit in season? Are we being productive for the vinedresser?

Chapter 3

PRECEDENT RESEARCH AND LITERATURE REVIEWS

Much thought by many has been given to the topic, "Paralysis in the Pew." The problem is widely recognized, and its research involves various authors from diverse areas and with varied audiences. I gathered information from the Internet, publications, and individuals, seeking personal as well as formal information and insight into the cause and possible cure for this spiritual malady. Fortunately, for this investigation, there were both people and parishes with the same problem, yet with the same passion for rectification. The research, readings, and retrieving of their reports proved both refreshing and rewarding.

To begin, I maintain that the model for full, participatory body ministry was given by the early Church in Acts 2:41–47. Authors Williams and Gangel concur.

> Here are some of the activities of the Early Church. They evangelized, baptized, learned doctrine from the apostles, fellowshipped, broke bread, prayed, saw signs and wonders, shared their belongings, gave to anyone who had need, met in the temple courts, ate meals together in homes, and praised God. These activities can be divided into the categories of

> worship, evangelism, education, fellowship, and ministry. Worship included baptism, the Lord's Supper, prayer, and praise. Evangelism resulted in people accepting the Gospel message. Education occurred as believers devoted themselves to the apostle's teaching. Fellowship took place through meeting and eating. Ministry describes how Christians met the needs of others.[23]

The quest, then, must be, "How do we engender full ministry when most of society is consumed with work, recreation, entertainment, traveling, and family?" In other words, how do Churches accomplish the task of full ministry when committed workers are so hard to identify, enlist, and develop?

The plight and pursuit is to get Church members committed to the work of the Lord through the work of the Church. Most of the work is done by a small percentage of the membership, while the greater percentage remains unresponsive or uncommitted. In this pursuit to enlist the uninvolved members in the necessary work of the Church, leadership cannot operate in what can only be considered a crisis management mode. That is, leaders cannot fill service positions of critical importance with persons who are not filled with the Spirit. Neither can leaders place individuals in serving capacities without gift suitability, appropriate skills, and adequate supervision.

> When people join a Church, we may take the opportunity to teach them how they can be involved in service. As we present various opportunities and enlist these people in some form of ministry, we should carefully follow the Spirit's leading. People can be challenged to find the right place of service in which they can both be fulfilled and contribute to the ministry in the

---

23. Dennis E. Williams and Kenneth O. Gangel, *Volunteering for Today's Church: How to Recruit and Retain Workers* (Eugene, OR: WIPF and Stock Publishers, 2004), 12–13.

> Church. When people choose not to serve, Church leaders do well to seek an understanding of the reasons. Many have too many commitments in other areas, while some just show no interest in serving. Perhaps both need to be challenged from a spiritual perspective. Watching how people invest their time and resources helps us know what they feel is important. This is what motivates them. Then we may challenge these people to identify and adopt biblical priorities which will bring spiritual fulfillment and satisfaction.[24]

One of the greatest weaknesses that afflicts the Church is allowing members who are uninvolved to remain uninvolved. "And active members do the voluntarily inactive members no service when they allow them to remain members of the Church, since membership is the Church's corporate endorsement of a person's salvation."[25] Attendance and activity are two important ways the Church can monitor one's relationship with Christ and His body. If a person is what I call a "shift member," the Church can neither adequately nor accurately assess an individual's relationship with Christ or with his Church. A shift member is one who is sporadic and is seldom in attendance or involved in Church activities. The Church in which I currently serve as pastor did not always have a full-time pastorate. Prior to my coming, the Church met every Sunday, but the pastoral Sundays were the second and the fourth Sundays of each month. The first, third, and fifth Sundays were for associate or guest ministers. Though every Sunday is now pastoral Sunday, some members still attend only twice a month on the first and third Sundays or on the second and fourth Sundays. Others come every other month or on occasion. Their involvement is as intermittent as their attendance. Shift members are neither consistent nor committed to Christ or to the Church. Their involvement, attendance, and activity

---

24. Williams and Gangel, *Volunteering*, 10.
25. Mark Dover, *What Is a Healthy Church?* (Wheaton, IL: Crossway Publishing, 2007), 97.

in the Church cannot be depended upon. The uninvolved member is not being condemned by the Church; they simply cannot be confirmed by the Church.

It is commonly understood that in most vocations, organizations, and relationships, inactivity or nonattendance results in dismissal. The Church is the one organization that allows its members simply to not attend, not be active in its endeavors, and not allocate to the Church and its mission, yet be counted as a member in "good standing." We must hold members accountable for both their attendance and their active involvement in the Church and its work. When members become more involved, membership becomes more meaningful. It will be more than membership *in name;* it will be membership *in fact!*

The following were sources of valuable information and insight into the problem of inactivity of Church members.

1. **Herbert W. Byrne, *Reclaiming Inactive Church Members.* Trafford Publishing, 2006.**

Byrne claims that one of the greatest problems Churches face today is a loss of membership. High on the list of causes for this situation is the failure of Churches to engage and retain the services of inactive members. I am offering various suggestions to solve this problem. I am providing not only advice but also illustrations of how local Churches have found solutions to this spiritual epidemic.

Understandably, I am interested in how and why the Church loses members. I found that loss in membership can be attributed to three principle areas: view, value, and vocation. In many instances, the leadership's view of members is an inequity of potentiality. There is a tendency to prefer those persons who are professional, positioned, and popular. Members who do not possess these attributes or accolades are often distanced, distracted, or dissuaded from duty.

Our point of view will often determine our value. Does the Church lose members because they do not feel valuable or valued? When someone is valued, they are noticed, named, and described as "necessary." Sadly, many members are overlooked in the society of the saints. Their names are never called. In many Churches, members are not known by names; they are known by seats. From the pulpit, I have, on occasions, mentioned members who were sick, going through crisis, or had a death in the family—calling them by name—only to see other members looking around and wondering who this person was. However, when the area where they regularly sat, the row and the seat, was pointed out, everyone knew who the person was.

Because of the view and the vocation, members are often not vocational. It is understood that members should volunteer and offer their services, but many are waiting to be approached and asked to be involved. This is the point Jesus makes in the parable of the lost coin in Luke 15:8–10. The coin was noticed, named, and needed. When the coin fell from the necklace, it was noticed. Oftentimes, members are absent and away for months before anyone inquires about their whereabouts or their condition. It is my contention that the coin was named because it was part of the set. The woman knew which piece had fallen; therefore, she knew the particular piece to be found. The coin was needed because ten was also the number of completion. Without that one piece, the set was not complete. In like manner, the church does not lose members; they fall because of how they are viewed or how little they are valued. Like the coin, however, when dropped, they fall within reach and can be easily retrieved if the Church responds rapidly and responsibly.

2. Mark S. Jones, *Reclaiming Inactive Church Members*. Broadman Press, 1988.

In his text, Jones gives what I call a medical approach to the problem of inactivity—giving the cause, the consequence, and the cure. His work addresses the process of inactivity with an analytical view of conjoining stage. After revealing the cause and the consequence, he proceeds with the cure, thus helping in the effort of becoming truly whole.

In his approach, Jones lists four major causes of inactivity:

1. Conflict. Conflict is virtually unavoidable in the local Church. It is also understood that conflict has been used as a reason for noninvolvement and inactivity for years. However, conflict is encountered not only in employment but in other routine encounters and environments of life, yet people remain active (involved, engaged) in those. There is conflict on the job, but they clock in every morning. There is conflict in the home, but they still live there. Though conflict is routinely "diagnosed" as a cause, it is, in reality, nothing more than a cop-out or evidence of a lack of personal commitment.

Whenever and wherever there is diversity, there is difference, and wherever there is difference, there is the likelihood of conflict. Conflict is often associated with disagreement or difference. When someone does not agree with others or does not acquiesce to their view, it can easily be interpreted as conflict. Conflict can lead to contention, and contention can quickly bring confusion within congregations. I believe conflict is a result of immaturity—spiritual or emotional. Perhaps the member has not reached the place in his or her spiritual growth to consider others and their opinions, which may offer a better view or outcome. It is the ignoring of the input of other individuals that fractures our fellowships and ruptures our relationships. When we are commonly concerned about reaching the common goal, one does not care who receives the credit—we do not see conflict because of differences; we see complementarity because of our common goals.

2. Unmet Expectations. Jones also suggests that members often come with the expectation of having their orders filled according to their own menus. When those expectations are not fulfilled, they become disgruntled, and inactivity is the common result. I believe this view is that of a consumer and not that of a customer. A customer chooses the place of dining based on his or her appetite. When a customer enters a restaurant, he or she is seated and given a menu. The menu lists the drinks, appetizers, entrees, and desserts that are served in that establishment. No customer can bring in his or her own menu and demand that the chef prepare a meal from it. They are to order from the menu provided. When a member becomes inactive because what they want is not on the menu, it is often diagnosed as unmet expectations. But in reality, the cause is that the person is egocentric—self-centered and self-seeking.

3. Lack of Affinity. Jones contends that Churches are composed of like-minded people of the same socioeconomic class and geographical area. So when the demographics change due to mortality, migrating relatives, or missed relationships, they lose their affinity and become inactive. I refer to this not as a lack of affinity but as a loss of allegiance. Although people unite with a local Church because of the reviews from the public and the relationships with the people, they should, above all else, be led by the Spirit to unite with a local Church. The primary purpose of Church membership is not to mingle with the members but to minister for the Master. When we base our involvement in the Church on people, we will work as long as they are there. When we base our involvement on the purpose of our membership, we will be involved regardless of the people. An uninvolvement in ministry results from members' caring more about their association with the members than they do about their allegiance to the Master.

4. Inability to Relate. According to Jones,

> Some members have a problem being satisfied in whatever Church they attend. This particular breed can hold consecutive memberships in a large number of Churches in a surprisingly short period of time. They are called "Church hoppers." In a category all to themselves, they are unable to get along with practically everyone. Members of this category seem to be misfits. The problems they complain about in the Church are actually problems they experience within themselves. They take the problems with them wherever they go. As a result they have a problem developing meaningful relationships with others.[26]

---

26. Mark S. Jones, *Reclaiming Inactive Church Members* (Nashville, TN: Broadman Press, 1988), 24.

Members want to fit in and feel a part of a Church. Some go out of their way trying to be accepted by certain members in order to gain a sense of belonging. While relating is important in a relationship, we must remember that relating to people is not forced but formulated. Whether they know it or not, they are already related because, as Paul said, "But now hath God set the members every one of them in the Body, as it hath pleased Him" (1 Corin. 12:18). Being an active part of the body, over time, each will be recognized, received, and respected. So if members are inactive, it is not because they do not fit; it is because they are not focused.

3. Jonathan Leeman. *Church Membership*. Crossway Publishing, 2012.

Jonathan Leeman emphasizes the critical importance of Church membership. In a time when this part of the Christian life is often neglected, Leeman builds a strong argument for the Church and the importance of being a member. He reminds us that Church is an obligation, not an option.

Church membership is critically important. Church is the place where a person substantively identifies with Christ and His body. Some want to operate under the banner of Christ in obscurity, rather than openly. Christians are publicly baptized to publicly identify themselves with the body of Christ. Remember, Jesus said, "No man, when he hath lighted a candle, putted it in a secret place, neither under a bushel, but on a candlestick, that they which come in may see the light" (Luke 11:33). Jesus also said, "Whosoever therefore shall be ashamed of Me and of My words in this adulterous and sinful generation; of him also shall the Son of Man be ashamed, when He cometh in the glory of His Father with the holy angels" (Mark 8:38).

Church is the place where the believer grows in Christ. Church both provides for and prepares the Christian for growth. The Church gives the believer support and opportunities to grow. That is why it is so important that Christians remain in one Church for extended periods of time and not Church-hop. Christians cannot grow if they are constantly moving. People who deal with plants, flowers, and trees know that you cannot grow a plant if you repot it every day. The plant must remain in one place in order to put down roots and be able to grow. Church is the place where this can happen.

Church is also the place where the believer can get involved with Christ and his work through the Church. Church provides both obligations and opportunities to make a difference in the life and in the labor of the Church. The gift, talent, skill, and ability are to be used in that part of the body where God has determined one should serve. A believer, therefore, should feel compelled and be committed to being involved in the local Church.

4. Thom S. Rainer. *I Am a Church Member.* B & H Publishing Group, 2013.

The work by Thom Rainer is like a fishing rod for the Church. It helps bait the line with the privilege of membership. It is a joy to be part of a fellowship where you can gather and grow as Christ intended. Rainer casts, as it were, a line into the waters of Scripture, simplicity, and practicality. He unapologetically reels us in with what is expected of those who join the body of believers.

There is an emphasis in this writing to not just *go to* Church but to *belong* to one—not just to attend but to be active. While membership has its privileges, it is a privilege to be a member of the Church. No other organization offers what this organism offers. Organizations offer earthly benefits and packages. Church membership offers both earthly and heavenly—eternal—rewards.

Rainer invites his readers to join him on a journey of both discovery and rediscovery, once again realizing the joy of church membership. At the end of this journey, he says,

> You will likely have a new or renewed attitude about your Church. You will learn the joy of being last instead of seeking to be first. Instead of being a whiner complaining about what's

wrong with your Church, you will be a unifier seeking what's best for your Church.[27]

5. **Gary McIntosh and Glen Martin. *Finding Them, Keeping Them: Effective Strategies for Evangelism and Assimilation in the Local Church.* Broadman Press, 1992.**

This work by McIntosh and Martin presents the reader with a before-and-after picture of responsibility for the believer. The Church is to reach the unsaved through evangelism, but once "enrolled," the Church has a responsibility to hold them. This is achieved through finding a place for them in the membership and in the ministry of the Church. I share the strategy of identification and inclusion. People need to identify with the people and feel included in the program. If people do not feel a part, they will not become a part.

The title alone assesses the agenda and assignment as an assembly. "Finding them" sends us out to seek the sinner. Our agenda is to evangelize the world—that is, carry the gospel to the world. The Great Commission is not "Wait," but "Go." We are "fishers of men." Fish do not leave the sea, totter through town, slide down our street, and leap into our frying pan. We have to go where they are, bait our hook, cast our line or net, pull them in, put them in a container, and carry them to our place. Jesus said, "For the Son of man is come to seek and to save that which was lost" (Luke 19:10).

"Fencing them and feeding them"—this is what "keeping them" entails. After we find them, our assignment is to keep them. We keep them by teaching them and training them. We keep them by watching over them and by working with them. Jesus was a keeper. Jesus said, "While I was with them in the world, I kept them in Thy Name: those that Thou gavest Me I have kept, and none of them is lost, but the son of perdition; that the Scripture might be fulfilled" (John 17:12).

"Finding them, keeping them" is the obligation of the Church. In

---

27. Rainer, *I Am A Church Member*, 6.

fact, the survival of the Church depends on it. The importance of this is observed in the occupation of James and John. Mark records, "And when He had gone a little further thence, He saw James the son of Zebedee, and John his brother, who also were in the ship mending their nets" (Mark 1:19). In the context of the text, the disciples saw a school of fish, cast their net, and caught the fish, but they could not contain the catch of fish. When they got the net to the ship, there was a decrease in the numbers of fish. They did not count as many in the ship as they had caught in the sea. Somewhere between the sea and the ship, some had slipped back into the sea.

Most would agree that the Church has taken in more members than can be seen. Somewhere between catching them in the street and counting them in the sanctuary, the Church has fallen in the numbers. Many have slipped back into their sins. The fall in the numbers can be attributed to a hole in the net. It was not the whole net, but one area—one part of the net had come loose. One part of the net had an opening. One section in the net had too much space. The fall in numbers can be attributed to a hole in the net. Membership studies call this "falling away" or "the revolving-door syndrome." These terms merely describe the hole in the net.

Scripture records that they were "mending their nets." The word *mending* is *katartízō* in Greek, which conveys the fundamental idea of putting something into its appropriate condition so it will function properly. The disciples were "mending their nets," preparing for a return to the sea and prevention of a loss of fish. They were trying to ensure that the next launch would be successful. As it was with the disciples, holding on to the catch in our nets should be our occupation.

Chapter 4

RESEARCH METHODOLOGY

For this project, I used three Primitive Baptist Churches—Christian Union Primitive Baptist Church, Mobile, Alabama; Indian Creek Primitive Baptist Church, Huntsville, Alabama; and Union Hill Primitive Baptist Church, Huntsville, Alabama—and four Missionary Baptist Churches—Bethlehem Missionary Baptist Church, Citronelle, Alabama; Central Missionary Baptist Church, Whistler, Alabama; Mt. Sinai Missionary Baptist Church, Whistler, Alabama; and Yorktown Missionary Baptist Church, Plateau, Alabama—which approximate in membership and in ministry of the Church where I serve.

The ministries used for the survey provide insight into the problem, as well as ideas on ways to improve the active percentage of member involvement. It was my intent to restrict the survey to Churches of similar size, belief, and depth of involvement to keep the findings fairly equitable and revealing.

The surveys were given to the pastors of each Church to decide how the survey would best serve their congregations. Each pastor acted individually in decisions about which groups would receive a survey or if surveys would be given on a volunteer basis. Elder Jeffrey T. Rainey, pastor of Christian Union Primitive Baptist Church, limited the surveys to approximately forty people, including leaders, volunteers, and inactive members. Elder Timothy M. Rainey, pastor of Indian Creek Primitive

Baptist Church, chose an adult Sunday School class consisting of both men and women between the ages of thirty and seventy to take the survey. Dr. Oscar L. Montgomery, pastor of Union Hill Primitive Baptist Church, asked the members who wanted to participate in the survey to remain after worship and complete it, and they turned it in upon completion. Rev. Joseph Laffiette, pastor of Bethlehem Missionary Baptist Church, chose a core group of the leadership staff to take the survey. Rev. Harry Pugh, pastor of Central Missionary Baptist Church, chose those who served in various leadership capacities as officers, in finance administration, and in religious education of the Church for this survey. Rev. Bernard Lambert, pastor of Mt. Sinai Baptist Church, did not engage the members in the survey. Instead, he offered an overseer's observation on the paralysis in the pew. Rev. Christopher Williams, pastor of Yorktown Baptist Church, used his inner office personnel for this survey.

The survey was titled, "The Ministry Survey." The full survey can be seen in Appendix A. The average Sunday worship attendance was eighty five. Twenty-five surveys were returned. The following questions were asked:

1. What is your age?
2. What is your gender?
3. How long have you been a member of your current Church?
4. What is the extent of your involvement?
5. Do you currently serve in a leadership role?
6. How would you generally describe your congregation?
7. How would you describe the level of stress experienced by your core group of leaders due to various demands of ministry?
8. How would you describe the distribution of tasks within your congregation?
9. How does low participation affect the level of stress among the core group leaders? What amount of stress does low participation have upon the stress levels of core group leaders?
10. Are the ministries of your Church able to accommodate the abilities, the gifts, and the talents of the membership?

11. Does the Church provide an atmosphere that encourages membership involvement?
12. Are there incentives and/or information made available for increased participation? What is the current level of effort made by the leadership to engage all members in meaningful ministry?
13. Does your Church have a mission and vision statement?
14. Is there a mechanism within your Church for communicating the mission vision and goals of your Church?
15. Do you sense that the members care about their Church image in the community?

The following table shows feedback followed by survey summaries for each Church.

Table 1. Survey answers from seven churches

	Christian Union	Indian Creek	Union Hill	Bethlehem	Central	Mt. Sinai	Yorktown
Survey Questions							
1. What is your age?							
1–11 years			–				
12–17 years			4				
18–25 years	1	1	1		1		
26–40 years	4	5	6	1	2		1
41–60 years	8	8	47	4	2		1
> 60 years	12	3	28	3			1
2. What is your gender?							
Male	5	3	37	2	3		1
Female	20	12	49	6	2		2
3. How long have you been a member of your current church?							
0–5 years	3	13	12				
6–10 years	4		8	2	1		1
> 10 years	18	4	66	6	4		2

4. What is the extent of your involvement?						
Low	5	1	8		1	1
Moderate	6	5	35	2	2	2
High	14	11	41	6	1	
Nonexistent						
5. Do you currently serve in a leadership role?						
Yes	14	6	47	6	4	
No	11	9	39	1		3
6. How would you generally describe your congregation?						
Evangelistic	5	5	22	1		
Sunday worship centered	16	12	37	6	4	
Missions oriented	4	6	33	3	1	
Linked by common culture in community		4	29	2		3
7. Describe level of stress experienced by core group leaders						
Nonexistent		2	4	1	3	
Low	13	4	24	1	1	1
Moderate	10	8	42	6	1	2
High	2	2	15			
8. Describe distribution of tasks within congregation						
80/20 (80% watch, 20% work)	17	9	54	2	5	3
50/50 (50% watch, 50% work)	3	5	18	6		
20/80 (20% watch, 80% work)	5	2	13			
9. How does low participation affect core leader stress?						
None	1	2	2		3	1
Low	5	3	17	1	2	
Moderate	11	4	39	4		
High	8	7	26	3		2
10. Does church accommodate member abilities, gifts, talents?						
Yes	19	14	71	7		3
No		1	6			
I don't know	6	2	7	1	5	

11. Does church provide atmosphere that encourages involvement?						
Yes	13	13	75	6	4	
No	12	3	3	2		3
I don't know		1	4		1	
12. Information made available and effort made to engage membership?						
Low	5	4	7			1
Medium	5	9	29	4	2	2
High	13	3	46	3	3	
I don't know	2	1	3			
13. Church has mission/vision statement?						
Yes	25	17	85	7	5	
No						3
I don't know						
14. Communicate mechanism for church goals?						
Yes	19	12	76	7	4	1
No	1	1			1	2
I don't know	5	4	3			
15. Do members care about church image in community?						
Yes	17	11	69	7	4	3
No	6	1	5	1		
Haven't thought about it	2	5	6			

Survey Summary: Christian Union Primitive Baptist Church, Mobile, Alabama

The responses in this survey have raised the covers and have revealed the conditions that will revolutionize our Church. First, among the twenty-five parishioners that returned the survey, 48 percent of the responses were from members sixty years of age and above. Perhaps this is the group that is most or more interested and most or more involved in the service and in the support of the Church. This percentage is an urgent call to reach, to recruit, and to relieve the seniors who are, presently, the longevity leaders and laborers carrying the load.

Second, 64 percent described our congregation as a (Sunday) worship center. This viewpoint explains the 20 percent involvement in evangelism and the 16 percent interest in missions. Sunday worship centers exhibit and employ devotional leaders, music ministry, hospitality, and preaching. So if the members are not officers, singers, ushers, greeters, or preachers, they perhaps concede to the notion that they have nothing to contribute and no role to play. Therefore, they come to be entertained rather than to be engaged. We have work to do in the areas of informing and inspiring individuals to be involved in the weekday ministries of our Church.

Third, the stress level varies depending on the commitment and on the concentration of the core. One member commented, "It makes a difference when there is maximum participation from all involved: leaders and members. When everyone does their part, it makes things run smoothly and will not tire out others. Ministry is not meant to be stressful. There is an inverse relationship between high participation and low stress levels."

Fourth, though 100 percent are aware of the mission statement of our Church, 76 percent acknowledge that there is a mechanism within our Church for communicating the mission, vision, and goal of our Church; 76 percent affirm that the ministries of our Church are able to accommodate the abilities, gifts, and talents of the membership; and 52 percent attest that incentives and information are made available for increased participation. Yet, 68 percent of the membership admits that 80 percent of the membership watches while 20 percent of the membership works.

This survey is a tool that will temper us to target, transition, and treat "paralysis in the pew."

Elder Jeffrey T. Rainey, Servant

Survey Summary: Indian Creek Primitive Baptist Church, Huntsville, Alabama

The participants in this survey are attendees of an adult Sunday School class consisting of both men and women between the ages of thirty and seventy. The glaring perception of those taking the survey suggests that increased participation of Church members is hindered because leadership fails to provide enough incentives for getting involved. It is clear that more must be done to make members aware of ministry opportunities through periodic dissemination of material about ministries as well as motivational pushes from the pulpit.

In this survey, insight was gathered regarding the core group. The class recognized that the Church's working membership is small: 80 percent watching, 20 percent working. Among the leadership, the stress level for the 20 percent is understood. Those not in leadership roles are not as privy to the magnitude of the stress and see the level as moderate.

It should also be noted that those who are not in leadership roles and who also have a low participation rate see the Church mostly as a worship center rather than a Church that is mission oriented and evangelistic. The lack of involvement clouds the view.

What was well documented in the survey is the good communication of the Church mission and vision. That sets the Church on good footing to correct the above.

Rev. Timothy M. Rainey, Senior Pastor

Survey Summary: Union Hill Primitive Baptist Church

This survey was compiled by Elder Jeffrey T. Rainey, a son of Union Hill Primitive Baptist Church, under supervision of Oscar L. Montgomery Sr., Pastor.

When a Church has good attendance, aggressive ministries, and accomplishable goals, it is easy to overlook the strain, the sacrifice, and the stress that the success is having on those who are serving. Of the surveys received, 54 percent are from members between the ages of forty and sixty. This age bracket usually comprises persons in the workforce who are parents and providers. They are the ones who have to drop off and pick up children, get the children to extracurricular activities, run errands, pay bills, still make Church meetings, support financially, and sacrifice for ministries.

Surprisingly, these are the one who do, give, and go the most and complain the least. This group is not stressed by the low participation of others, which implies that they love their Church and get joy from their ministry involvement. This seems to be the case because according to the surveys received, 76 percent of the participants have been members for ten years or more. What adds to the success is the gift of cooperation among the core group. They seem to know how to compliment and to commend one another to commit to the completion.

Though the membership of this Church is larger than others', the ratio of participation is 80/20. So the larger the congregation is, the greater the challenge is to involve members in ministry to combat and to cure the "paralysis in the pew."

Survey Summary: Bethlehem Missionary Baptist Church, Citronelle, Alabama

This survey has unearthed a misunderstanding of the true culture of our Church among some of those who are in leadership roles. I noticed a discrepancy in answers when questioned concerning the stress level of core leaders over low membership participation. It seems as if those who are actively engaged in doing the work understand that low membership participation causes a high amount of stress, while those who are engaged only moderately answered that the stress level was low. This question and the varied answers that were received revealed the need to communicate better the hardship that is experienced by key leaders when membership participation is low. I am also inclined to believe that perhaps in the few areas that membership participation is low, it is directly attributed to the fact that the leaders in those areas have failed to communicate to the members in that area of ministry the importance they play in achieving the overall mission of the Church.

The other interesting thing I noticed was that there was a disconnect also with question eight, which concerned the equal distribution of tasks within the congregation. There were some members who answered that involvement was 50 percent watching and 50 percent working, while some answered 80 percent watching and 20 percent working. Overwhelmingly, those who are themselves less engaged seem to mark 50/50, while those who bear the greater share of the load marked 80/20! This also exposes that those who feel that the tasks are shared 50/50 are uninformed concerning the true nature of participation in the Church. I find this extremely helpful because it gives me the demographics to educate leaders on the true conditions, as well as to formulate a plan to “evangelize” members, so to speak, and to engage and encourage members who make up the remaining inactive percentile. I believe also that there may be a misunderstanding of what active membership is in our Church. The answers also show that some seem to have mistaken regular Sunday attendance as active, engaged participation. As troubling as this is, it provides a bird’s-eye view of the problem and allows me an opportunity to pray and implement some things that can be done to cure “Paralysis in the Pew,” or at least greatly reduce the malady at the Bethlehem Church. These are just a few observations that were made as a result of this survey. If you have any further questions, please feel free to contact me, and thanks for the opportunity to contribute.

Dr. Joseph P. Laffiette II

Survey Summary: Central Missionary Baptist Church, Whistler, Alabama

The core group for this survey is those who serve in various leadership capacities with ages fluctuating from twenty-five to sixty-five, both men and women. Those who were surveyed serve as officers, in finance administration, and in religious education of the Church. It is interesting to note that the notion of 80 percent watching and 20 percent working was common among this group and none seem to feel too hindered by the nonworkers but agree it could have a hindering effect on growth of the membership. There will always be some differences of opinions because everyone interprets what they see or seems to understand differently. I think that this is due to their individual perceptions of how each one sees his or her position.

They all agree that the Church has a "mission statement," but there are some differences in judgment about the mission work. There is a majority opinion about the stress level but differences about the gifts. This is an indication that there must be more done to inform the membership of the importance of ministry work. As a leader, one would think, there should not have been any "I don't knows" in this survey simply because a leader in a core group should find it validating to answer "yes" or "no" due to their involvement; nevertheless, it is always surprising to see and hear what the laity really think about what we as leaders take for granted that they should know.

It is with trepidation that I note that the majority sees a worship center and not a Church that is mission oriented and evangelistically operating. This reason alone will cause a lack of growth in the pew. This type of outlook causes stagnation, and this will become a product of inactivity and immobility due to the privation of knowledge. This survey is the attestation that the Church needs to implement a strategy to inform the membership of the importance to understand and act upon the Church's mission and vision statements so that paralysis in the pew can become nonpromotional.

Dr. Harry B. Pugh Sr., Senior Pastor

Survey Summary: Mt. Sinai Missionary Baptist Church, Whistler, Alabama

The pastor of Mt. Sinai decided not to give the survey to members. He chose, from an overseer perspective, to reflect on the preventive measures of the Mt. Sinai Missionary Baptist Church. Despite the efforts and the endeavor to eradicate this epidemic, it still exists.

Survey revision information

The following are additions to the questions answered by Pastor Bernard Lambert.

Question eight addition: Each deacon is responsible for what is called a ward. The deacon who is assigned a ward is responsible for all the members in a geographical area. His wife is assigned to be his secretary; she is responsible for making contact with the members in their ward. The deacons are required to make a written report of their members at the year-end conference.

Question ten addition: Mission department, Matron Department, Youth Department, Laymen All Men's Group, Mass Choir, Youth and Young Adult Choir, Male Chorus, Senior Citizen Group, Mothers Board, Deaconess Ministry.

Question twelve addition: Christian Education Director and Superintendent is responsible for keeping the Church informed. Each fifth Sunday, we have group study session for adults. Special topics are chosen for discussion at this time such as evangelism, Church attendance, fellowship, accountability, Christian ethics, Church etiquette, and so on.

Question fourteen: The new member class provides information to the new members: the various ministries within our Church, what we believe as a Baptist Church, method of finance, Articles of Faith, and doctrines. A Membership Guidebook is made available to all members. This book provides each member with imperative information, such as annual days, staff job descriptions, information concerning the pastor, and what we offer the members at our Church.

Rev. Bernard Lambert Sr., Pastor

Survey Summary: Yorktown Missionary Baptist Church

The audience for this survey consists of both men and women between the ages of twenty-five and seventy-five. The perception of those surveyed suggests that increased participation of Church members is hindered because leadership fails to provide enough incentives for getting involved. Involvement must begin with the pulpit and then move downward to and throughout the pews.

It is abundantly clear that those involved in the survey were speaking on the behalf of the majority of the Church. With this in mind, it again becomes the Church's leadership responsibility to correct the problem and become the leaders that God has established us to be. We can do this by:

- Recognizing those that are in leadership
- Reaching the leadership through education
- Holding those that are in leadership responsible
- Replacing those that are inadequate
- Rehearsing the process continually

Contrary to popular belief, Church problems are not created in the congregation, but rather they are created in leadership. When we fix the leadership situation, then we can work on the congregation. The survey helps bring to the forefront the fact that those that are not in leadership, and some that are, have low participation rates because they see the Church as a place to worship and not a place of worship and service. Much work and prayer must be done to correct this.

The favorable portion of the survey consists of a strong family and community relationship that had ventured over into the Church. Yet it has also caused separation within the Church between different families.

"Paralysis in the Pew" is a proper statement that we as pastors and leaders with God's help and leadership must face head on. With God we can correct this situation.

Rev. Christopher L. Williams Sr., Pastor

Chapter 5

RESEARCH FINDINGS

It was my intention to both discover and to disclose the disease of congregational inactivity in the body of Christ. I am convinced that Christians are both cognizant and capable of the calling the Lord has placed on their lives, yet far too many choose not to commit to, cooperate with, or contribute to the ministry of the Church. This spiritual perplexity moved me to seek after solutions. In this quest, I inquired of other Churches by way of a survey for information, insight, and ideas. Needless to say, I was appreciative of the responsibility taken and the responses given by each of the selected Churches. And, though not overly surprising, the results were nevertheless quite revealing.

First, preparation for the survey itself revealed that some members of the targeted congregations were not comfortable with committing their true thoughts to paper. This in itself is an indication that some people do not want to get involved or even to draw attention to themselves by taking part in a written survey, which is merely a study of the present in order to improve the future. I am convinced that most members want better for their Churches but feel at risk of being labeled, even targeted, by others for their feelings. This is easy to understand, for some Churches gave the survey only to a select or limited group, whereas the Christian Union Primitive Baptist Church and the Union Hill Primitive Baptist Church gave the survey to the whole of the Church. Even with this openness, however, only about 16 percent of the members of Christian Union Primitive Baptist Church and approximately 13 percent of the members of Union Hill Primitive Baptist Church actually submitted a completed survey. This statistic alone speaks volumes.

Some members did not care enough about the obligation and operation of their Churches to take ownership by being open with their opinions and forthright with their observations. Silence contributes nothing; silence gives credence to both right and wrong. There was a television commercial showing injustice being done, and when someone spoke up, it changed both the decision and the direction of action. The intent was to highlight "the power of one voice." In my travels, on numerous occasions I have noticed signs throughout various airports encouraging sign-readers to action: "If you see something, say something." The Church may need a few of these signs posted.

Second, research revealed that among the surveys returned, the larger percentage of the members responding were between the ages of forty and sixty. Understandably, this group comprises the cream of the crop as far as volunteerism and activity. They are your professionals, your payers, your leaders, and your parents. And though they generally have the most to offer and are key to the overall ministry and function of the Church, perhaps there is a need to recruit members between the ages of eighteen and forty years to help lighten the load of those members serving during their prime years. Even more, there is a very real need to incorporate the seniors, who have blazed the trail and may now feel overlooked or left out.

Because the members between forty and sixty are, for all intents, the main shareholders of the Church, those in the age group below them may feel they simply do not measure up to "the standard," while the group above may feel their say no longer matters. A way to make all members feel important and have an avenue for input must be created.

Third, with the exception of Indian Creek Primitive Baptist Church and the Yorktown Baptist Church, the majority of the members who returned surveys have held membership for ten or more years. If there is inactivity among this group, it stands to reason that both pastor and parishioner have failed to both enlist and to encourage involvement, or we have allowed their stubbornness to silence their voices.

Normally, senior leadership expects the longevity laborers and the senior servants to be the benchmark for believers, the example for everyone, the model for members, the pattern for parishioners, and the standard for the saints. By relegating the tenured members to be on "seat ministry" rather than serving ministry, the Church does not strengthen its appeal for involvement. The Church must make the tenured members feel responsible for the success or the failure of those who are following them. My leadership motto is, "Leaders are examples for followers, not excuses for failures."

Fourth, question six of the survey reveals high identification with the description of the Sunday worship-centered congregation. I was particularly seeking answers to the questions: "Why are members comfortable with just coming to Church?" "Why are members satisfied with merely sitting in the sanctuary?" "Why are members meeting just to maintain their membership?" Along with these, the author was seeking answers to the questions: "Why are Christians not contributing to the Church?" "Why are the saints not serving in the service?" "Why are the members not ministering for the Master?"

It is not due to the fact that there is nothing to be done! Jesus said, "The harvest truly is plenteous, but the laborers are few" (Matt. 9:37). If one would simply preview the many and varied ministries within the scope and vision of the Church, one would see a tremendous need for laborers. There are needs all around. There is work to be done. There are vacancies to be filled. There is more to do and to be a part of in the Church than simply singing and ushering. There are other ministries awaiting ministers.

The Sunday worship-centered view may be one reason for the large percentage of uninvolved members. To work in worship means you have to preach, pray, sing, speak, and usher. If people do not have stage security and stamina, they feel inferior and insignificant and choose simply to be idle. The reason for this kind of thinking is that we have the wrong idea of what the work of the Church truly is. There is a widespread concept today that the real work of the Church is getting together and having a great meeting on Sunday mornings where we enjoy learning from the Scriptures and fellowshipping with one another. The thinking is that the people who lead these meetings have certain gifts. They have to keep everything in order. Others in the congregation look at them and say, "That is the work of the Church. I can't do any of those things. Therefore, I really have no part to play in the Church." But that is not the work of the Church at all.

The work of the Church is to heal the brokenhearted of the world, to give deliverance to the captives, to open the eyes of the blind, and to preach the good news to the poor and despairing of heart. The body of Christ is in the world to encourage, strengthen, and help people; to deliver them from guilt, loneliness, and the misery of sin; and to set them free from the bondage of foul tempers and evil habits as well as all the rack and ruin of life. That is what the work of the Church is. The work does not go on "in here." The work goes on "out there"!

Church leaders must both expose their members to and educate their members about the many features and functions within the body of Christ. There is more to the body than what eyes can see. There are more important faculties and functions inside the body that are vital. In fact, without the workings behind the scene, the body would not be able to perform outwardly. Members must be made aware of their vital roles, and though roles may be played behind the scenes or out of the sight of others, they are not inferior or insignificant; they are vitally important.

More importantly, question six of the survey—"How would you generally describe your congregation?"—helps identify the core value of the Church. The question was said to be confusing for some of the members of the Union Hill Primitive Baptist Church, so some of the members taking the survey marked multiple answers. Variable responses given when one viewpoint is requested indicates that the core value has not been clearly defined or the members are not sure of the vision or the mission of the Church. No one Church can be a spiritual jack-of-all-trades. No one Church can do everything or be everything for all. Each Church must identify its role and desired representation as a local body. I personally appreciate the view of Aubrey Malphurs when he says the pastor and Church leaders must return to the basics and dig deep. He writes that they must

> Ask important and fundamental questions, such as, Why are we here? Who are we? What drives us? What are we supposed to be doing? … Instead, far too many well-intentioned pastors find a ministry that God is blessing somewhere, attend its pastors' conference, and attempt to replicate its model back home.… These pastors are trying to franchise someone else's model. And the problem with franchising Church models is that what works in one part of the country does not necessarily work in another part of the country.[28]

A Church must discover and define its passion. What will the Church concentrate on, center on, and commit to? If the interest is the membership, the Church will be attentive, affectionate, and accountable for each member. If the interest is the message, the Church will emphasize listening to, learning, and living the Word. If the interest is the ministry, the Church will acknowledge, address, and alleviate the ailments in the assembly. If the interest is the mission, the Church will evangelize the lost within the community. Whatever the interest, the Church should strive to be efficient, effective, and excellent in emotions, expressions, and efforts.

John C. Maxwell, in his book entitled *The 21 Indispensable Qualities of a Leader*, says, "Everything rises and falls on leadership."[29] This perspective reflects the conviction of Christopher L. Williams Sr., the pastor of Yorktown Mission Baptist Church. Pastor Williams concluded, "The perception of those surveyed suggests that increased

---

28. Aubrey Malphurs, *Advanced Strategic Planning* (Grand Rapids, MI: Baker Books, 2005), 28.

29. John C. Maxwell, *The 21 Indispensable Qualities of a Leader* (Nashville, TN: Thomas Nelson Press, 1999), ix.

participation of Church members is hindered because leadership fails to provide enough incentives for getting involved. Involvement must begin with the pulpit and then move downward to and throughout the pews."

Fifth, the surveys revealed the level of stress experienced by the core group of leaders due to various demands of ministry. Even the 80 percent watching and 20 percent working ratio was moderate among the majority of the workers. I contend that one will either worry more than he or she works or work more than he or she worries. This makes it personal. People have been heard to say, "You can't worry about them (the uninvolved); the work has to be done." So they are more focused on what has to be done than they are on who is not contributing. These workers should be commended, congratulated, and compensated with our accolades, our acknowledgements, and our appreciation. Support minimizes stress and maximizes spirit.

There is, however, a need to communicate our stress. Sometimes, workers can be walking time bombs waiting to explode. When people serve without sharing what is worrying or weighing on them in their work, this can manifest in an explosive way. Excess stress is often silent and sneaky. It can be triggered by a word, it can be set off during work, and it can be caused to explode from an otherwise unconscious expression. Dr. Joseph Laffiette of the Bethlehem Missionary Baptist Church of Citronelle, Alabama, said in his survey summary,

> This question and the varied answers that were received revealed the need to communicate better the hardship that is experienced by key leaders when membership participation is low. I am also inclined to believe that perhaps in the few areas that membership participation is low, it is directly attributed to the fact that the leaders in those areas have failed to communicate to the members in that area of ministry the importance they play in achieving the overall mission of the Church.

Sixth, the surveys reveal that the vision statements, the involvement, the encouragement, and the individual Church's ability to accommodate the needs, abilities, gifts, and talents of its membership does not guarantee that members will become involved. Question twelve—"Are there incentives and/or information made available for increased participation?"—should incite us as well as inspire us to increase the information being made available to get more people involved. Elder Timothy M. Rainey, the senior pastor of Indian Creek Primitive Baptist Church of Huntsville, Alabama, expressed in his survey summary,

> The glaring perception of those taking the survey suggests that increased participation of Church members is hindered because leadership fails to provide enough incentives for getting involved. It is clear that more must be done to make membership aware of ministry opportunities through periodic dissemination of material about ministries as well as motivational pushes from the pulpit.

This requires preparation, patience, and prayer. Our preparation removes the excuses of the uninvolved. The member should not be able to say, "The Church does not have a place for me to work." Rather, the Church should be able to say, "We have a place for you to work, but you will not accept it." Our patience waits on the seed planted to bring forth a harvest. Our prayers keep us hopeful and keep us from giving up on people in their present predicaments.

Finally, the surveys reveal that the members surveyed care about their Churches' images in the community, but this appears to be true more in theory than in reality. None of the surveyed Churches had a high percentage in the characterization of their Church as evangelistic, as mission oriented, or as community-linked. We must admit that our demographics have changed. No longer do we have community Churches. Most Church attendees drive past five or more Churches each week before they arrive at their membership Church. A common comment is that we drive in, drive by, and drive away from the communities where our Churches are located.

We must reconcile in the hearts and minds of our membership that the building is for meeting, but the body is for ministering. The body cannot continue to come to a building without being moved to bless its boundaries. The neighborhood where the body meets should be better. Crime should decrease where the body meets. Immorality should be minimized where the body meets. We say we care, but do we care about our property and our possessions more than we care about the people? We must pray that God will give us a passion for souls.

Conclusion

The surveys have uncovered and unveiled the undercurrents that run beneath the surface of our undertakings. The tasks, the tactics, and the tools have become transparent through these surveys. I am convicted, convinced, and confident that cooperation and commitments will come to our Churches as a result of our implementation of this information.

Chapter 6

CONCLUSIONS AND RECOMMENDATIONS

The Church has many active, applicable, and available ministries for the increase of the membership, but the great percentage of the members are neither enrolled nor engaged in ministry. As a result, a few members keep the Church body functional, while the majority of the members of the church body fail to function because of "paralysis."

Church leaders are well aware of the 80/20 rule, where 20 percent of the people do 80 percent of the work, while 80 percent of the people sit quietly in the pew, seemingly content to do nothing—contributing little to the life and function of their local Church body. But are they truly content, or are they simply uninvolved because no one has asked them to contribute? Involving the uninvolved in ministry and fellowship is one of the greatest challenges in the Church today. Many people will say they do not have the time. While this may appear to be a legitimate excuse, it is not the sole answer. Life and reality show us that we have time for the things we truly value. We will often repeat activities in which we are fulfilled and make meaningful, even costly, contributions to these activities, even if it involves a degree of sacrifice.

> Many people drop out of Church because they are self-centered, concerned with their own ways and consumed with this world. This leads them to downgrade the importance of the Church and spiritual things and thereby results in the tendency to drop out of the Church. Unregenerate hearts have little power for change. Churches often fail to hold such people or to reach them because they do not take seriously the divine way of doing things revealed in the Word of God, leading Churches to evangelism, instruction, worship, fellowship and service."[30]

Perhaps value is the key to vocation. In Luke 15:3–7, the shepherd valued the lost sheep, so he left the ninety-nine and launched a search for the one. In Luke 15:8–10, the woman valued the lost coin, so she lit a candle and swept the house until it was found. In Luke 15:11–24, the father valued the prodigal son, so he ran to welcome him and threw a coming-home celebration. When people value their careers, they will perform their tasks. When people value their relationships, they will discharge their responsibilities. When people value their Churches, they will serve and support them. Value is perhaps the greatest key to vocation.

Value is our appraisal, our assessment, and our appreciation of individuals and involvement. Value is marked by mastery, mileage, and maturity. The immature or infant value system is not the same as the adult's. Infants are careless with things that are actually serious and significant because their view of them is immature—they do not view them as being important. Infants handle things with a sense of simplicity. They do not know how valuable documents can be; therefore, they will tear them up. They do not know how sentimental keepsakes are; therefore, they will play with them like they are toys. They do not know how important jobs are, so they will selfishly make parents late for work. The infant's value system is not the same as the adult's. It is my contention that is the case of many Christians in the Church.

30. Byrne, *Reclaiming Inactive Church Members*, 25.

Some Christians are infants and immature in the faith. They do not value the church as do the mature Christians. This, too, may well be a cause for individuals' being inactive or members' not being involved in the ministry of the Church. They do not value it for they do not recognize the true value of their ministry to the Church or the ministry of the Church as the body of Christ. If they are to become involved in the ministry of the Church, this value must be instilled in them. Again, value is perhaps the greatest key to vocation.

The value systems of our country, our Churches, our communities, and Christianity as a whole are crumbling. More specific, the doctrine, decorum, and duties of the Church are diminishing. In doctrine, our stand against sin is being compromised. In decorum, our behavior and our compromised lifestyles are being adopted, accepted, and accommodated. In duty, our obligation to serve and to support that which is eternally valuable has become an option. We have paralysis in the pew because of a low value or no value for the ministry or for the Church. Value is perhaps the greatest key to vocation.

To instill and to increase value in Church members, leadership must identify the cause, illuminate the condition, and implement the cure for this paralysis.

I. The Cause of Paralysis

Physically, paralysis is caused by damage to the central nervous system. If a body member is not responding to the request of the head, that body member is disconnected, disfunctional, or disoriented. These situations are caused by incidents, injuries, or illnesses. As a result, the body member does not discharge its duties. In like manner, spiritual paralysis is caused by any of the following:

1. The Risk Factor

Many members are reluctant to get involved and to take part because they are afraid of not being approved, accepted, and appreciated by leadership or the other members. Rather than feel or be rejected, they remove themselves from the work altogether. The risk causes many to not be involved in the ministry of the Church.

2. The Requirement Factor

Many members are not involved because of their schedules for work and for family. To be involved will interrupt and interfere with their plans and their time. Also, to be involved will mean being under scrutiny. Most people do not like answering to anyone or being accountable for what they do. They do not take well to being corrected or being critiqued. For them, it is added and unnecessary pressure. Furthermore, if they arc involved, service will be expected. Many do not want to be in a position of being depended upon. Requirements cause many to be uninvolved in the ministry of the Church.

3. The Reality Factor

Many are not involved because they are aloof. They are distant and indifferent. They do not feel a part, so they do not want to be a part. Others are not involved because of some ailment. They feel that their illness incapacitates them from being involved. Others are not involved because of age. Some are thought to be too young, while others feel they are too old. The young are told their time has not come, and the elderly are told their time has passed. These realities cause many to not be involved in the ministry of the Church.

II. The Condition of Paralysis

Paralysis is a state, a shape, and a situation that causes saints to be the following:

1. Inferior

Many are not involved because because they feel they do not measure up to the example or the expectations of others.

2. Idle

Many are like an idling engine. The motor is running and gas is being used, but there is no motion. The car sits idle and still. When a member of the body is paralyzed, he or she is still a part of the body and and is receiving the required substances as others are, yet he or she is yielding no response.

3. Ignorant

People may not be aware that opportunities exist. They look around, think that everything is going well, and assume there's no need for help. Change their thinking. Let members know how it would ease the load for others if more became involved.

4. Insensitive

While members are paralyzed, they give no utterance or urgency for their useless state. The success or the failure of the ministry does not have an effect on them.

III. The Cure for Paralysis

Many have recovered from physical paralysis through treatment, therapy, and time. I believe spiritual paralysis can be remedied through the following:

1. Targeting People

Leaders must be intentional as they seek out the uninvolved. Being intentional includes believing that individuals are important and that we are not recruiting people only to fill positions or to increase our numbers. We are doing so with the intentional mind-set that every follower of Christ is gifted with a spiritual gift or gifts and can contribute in a way that benefits the entire body.

Believing every person has both a place and a purpose in the body of Christ, the Church would be remiss by neglecting to be intentional in searching for and calling out those who will not always stand in the front of the line. The entire body will suffer and the individual will be unfulfilled as a disciple of Christ Jesus.

Personal contact. Many times, the general or more generic announcement or approach is not effective. Some need the personal, one-on-one approach. It is often far better to get people by themselves to interact with them. When you are face to face with a person, you can ask questions and receive personal answers. The chances are far greater for receiving a positive reaction and response from him or her when this is done. Personal contact is perceived as being very much preferred.

Penned communication. When people go to the mailbox and see personal correspondence from the Church, they are generally excited over the idea that time and thought went into that effort to reach them. It is even more effective when the pastor writes and addresses a letter and signs it personally.

Provoking challenge. When we see potential in people, we should bring it to their attention and encourage them to offer and to operate in their gift, talent, ability, or skill.

2. Timed Participation

> Timed participation is based on three things: time, task, and trust. Williams and Gangle, in *Volunteering for Today's Church*, write about these three. The first is time.
>
> One solution to the crisis in volunteers is to have more people serve with smaller time commitments. If a small percentage of a congregation does most of the work, Churches should try to increase this percentage by spreading the work load around. Look beyond the few who presently serve to the many who attend Church but do not contribute their time and effort. This is the pool of potential servants you need to penetrate. They need to be approached prayerfully, challenged to serve, and offered training and assistance in their new tasks.[31]
>
> Williams and Gangel next write about task.
>
> The professional staff should not do all the work of ministry. The professional staff must provide the leadership that equips and trains all of God's people for some kind of service. When professionals do take over the ministry, they keep other people whom God has gifted from serving. Two problems result. The professional staff will be overworked because they do not share the load. And people will become either bitter or indifferent to the Church if they do not have an opportunity to serve and use the gifts God has given them.[32]

Ronald W. Richardson, in his book titled *Creating a Healthier Church*, uses the example of "over- and underfunctioning":

---

31. Dennis E. Williams and Kenneth O. Gangel, *Volunteering for Today's Church* (Eugene, Oregon: WIPF and Stock Publishers, 2004), 10.

32. Williams and Gangel, *Volunteering for Today's Church*, 19–20.

Overfunctioning happens when one person takes increasing amounts of responsibility for the functioning of one or more other people. Overfunctioners can take over the thinking, feeling, or actions of the underfunctioners. As the underfunctioner does less in one or more of these three areas, the overfunctioner does more. As a consequence, the overfunctioner looks more responsible, healthy, mature, and adequate, and the underfunctioner looks less so.

Overfunctioners tend to think they "know" what is best for others, and they often think they have better solutions for the dilemmas of others. While they often do have many competencies, the fact that their strength is used in the service of anxiety usually nullifies what can be useful in their abilities.

Underfunctioners will be slow to claim their competence in the presence of overfunctioners. They will tend to act as if they don't know how to do much of anything. It is easier just to be dependent and let others worry about our wants and seek ways to fulfill them for us.

The more people overfunction in the Church, the more all suffer from issues of confused responsibility. Overfunctioners need to learn how to distinguish between what is their responsibility and what is the responsibility of others, and then they need to let go of things that they are not really responsible for. Underfunctioners will take more responsibility and do their job only if and when they begin to feel anxious about it being done.[33]

Williams and Gangel address the third factor, trust:

Leaders who try to do everything themselves or do not trust others with ministry responsibilities usually are poor delegators

---

33. Ronald W. Richardson, *Creating a Healthier Church: Family Systems Theory, Leadership, and Congregational Life* (Minneapolis, MN: Fortress Press,1996), 133–135.

and weak in helping others use their gifts. Perhaps they feel that jobs will not be done adequately and the work of the Church will be placed at risk. Indeed, this may happen when tasks are not explained or supervised properly. People who do not delegate or who delegate poorly are usually limited to smaller Church ministry opportunities they can personally control.[34]

3. Tailored Programs

Tailored garments are made according to a person's size, weight, and height. The author contends that duties should be designed, functions should be fitted, ministry should be measured, service should be sized, and tasks should be tailored to the individuals we are interested in involving. Therefore, programs should be tailored to pursue and to procure persons in the work of the Church. I recommends the following:

> *Surveying parishioners*. Many are in Church and, after many years, still seeking God's will for their lives. They claim they do not know what it is God would have them do. It is my belief that God is the greatest employer and has a place and a purpose for everyone He brings into the Kingdom. People do not work on a job for years without knowing their job placements or the job descriptions. They have a gift and need to unwrap it, uncover it, open it up, and put it into use. Leaders must help them discover and develop it. One way to know if one is serving in one's gifted area is that one is comfortable, confident, content, and celebrative in what one is doing.
>
> Many people do not know what they are good at doing. Spiritual gift inventories should be made available. Perhaps a class that helps people count their many abilities, discover their passions, examine their experiences, and consider their personalities as they consider various ways to serve should be

34. Williams and Gangel, *Volunteering for Today's Church*, 36–37.

offered. Membership assessment surveys to determine abilities and areas of ministry for each can be given. The time must be taken to instill the importance of each member's ideas, input, and involvement. The needs of the congregation must be highlighted, and a discussion of how ministering will address, assist, and alleviate those needs must be had.

A ministry fair could be offered. A ministry fair provides exposure to ministry opportunities. At the fair, each ministry could prepare a display to communicate to the congregation what that ministry is all about, how it fits into the mission statement of the Church, and its current needs.

The author penned and provided a description for each ministry in the Church. When people inquire about the duties and the discharges of that ministry, they are given a handout with the requested information to make an intelligent decision about the ministry of their personal interest and potential involvement.

Series preaching. The power of the preacher or pastor is his voice. That is what preaching entails: "*Preaching* is 'the spoken communication of divine truth with a view to persuasion.'"[35] Accepting this as a sufficient definition, we notice that it covers the three points of preaching with which we are chiefly concerned in a sermon, namely, its matter, its manner, and its motive. As to (1) the matter of this communication, it is *divine truth*—what to preach, (2) the manner of this communication, it is divine truth *spoken*—how to preach, and (3) the motive of

---

35. Thomas Harwood Pattison, *The Making of a Sermon* (Whitefish, MT: Kessinger Publishing, LLC, 2009), 3. *The Making of a Sermon* was originally published in 1898, and this quote was included in course materials from "Expository Preaching I" offered at Birmingham Theological Seminary, in Birmingham, Alabama.

this communication, it is divine truth spoken *with a view to persuasion*—why we preach.[36]

Series preaching provides clarity, continuity, and centrality to the topic and to the target being taught. I recommend the sermon series "The Ideal Church Member," an excellent series on Barnabas. The series illuminates the importance of involvement of individuals in ministry.

Sermon 1: Barnabas Shared His Fortune, Acts 4:32–37. Barnabas was the ideal church member. How seldom do we hear his name mentioned in sermons or studies? Yet he is one of the noblest of New Testament heroes. He gave his material possessions to the ministerial personnel for the multitude's provision. As a result, the shortage was solved because "neither was there any among them that lacked" (Acts 4:34). Not every person of means is a person of ministry (consider the rich young ruler in Mark 10:17–22, the rich farmer in Luke 12:16–21, and Dives, meaning "rich man" in Luke 16:19–31). Barnabas was such a man. Because of the liberality of his spirit, there was no lack among the saints.

Sermon 2: Barnabas Supported the Friendless, Acts 9:26–28. God directs some people to unite with our Church who want to belong to a body. They want to fit in the fellowship. They want to be involved with individuals. They want to be a part of a people. Yet, when they arrive, they are blocked by believers who will not let people in their company, conversation, or circle. They behave as if they have nothing in common. They will not be friendly to them or have any fellowship with them. They will not act favorably toward them. They behave as if they are foreigners. Sometimes Church leaders are not willing to give people a chance. Sometimes all folks need is someone to believe

---

36. Michael E. Reese, "Expository Preaching I," course syllabus from Birmingham Theological Seminary, Birmingham, Alabama, http://birminghamseminary.org/wp-content/uploads/2012/03/PT5722-Reese.pdf

in them! That is what Barnabas did. Barnabas did the ideal thing—he gave Saul a chance. We need someone to support the friendless. We do not know what God has blessed a person with that may in turn benefit the body of believers. So do not slight or shun people, but support them.

Sermon 3: Barnabas Strengthened the Flock, Acts 11:19–25. When the new church was formed in Antioch in Acts 19–21, the great work soon reached Jerusalem. The Church leaders in Jerusalem had a responsibility to "shepherd" the scattered flock, so the elders commissioned Barnabas to go to Antioch to help this infant Church (vs. 22–23). When churches or Christians are in their initial state or infant stage, they need immediate support. Because this is such an important service, we should identify saints who can influence spiritually. The Jerusalem Church dispatched Barnabas to *strengthen the flock*. The need was sensed, and the decision was made to seek help. The only question was about who should be secured. A unique person was needed—a person who not only had a Jewish background but who also knew the Greek language and culture and could relate to both Gentile and Jew alike. The person also needed to be fearless and bold in his witness for Christ because of the godless, immoral society of Antioch.

Barnabas knew such a man: Saul of Tarsus. So he set out to find him. The word *seek* (*anazēteō*) means to search for, to search back and forth, up and down; to make a thorough search.[37] Paul had been busy throughout Syria and Cilicia preaching about Christ (Gal. 1:21), and apparently Barnabas had difficulty finding him. Barnabas would have some concern about Paul's whereabouts but was determined to find him, though it would involve some searching. But note—he knew God's will, so he

---

37. Practical Word Studies in the New Testament, Page 1813
Copyright © 1998, by Alpha-Omega Ministries, Inc. All rights reserved. Database © 2014 WORD*search*.

did not give up the search. He kept searching until he found God's choice.

Barnabas was wise in this attitude. It pays to diligently search for the right one. Paul was worth all the time and effort required to find him. The same is true with Churches looking for a pastor, with young people looking for a mate, and with employers looking for employees. Do not take just anything that comes along. Search until you find the right one.

Barnabas was sent to strengthen the saints. When he strengthened them, he secured them by securing Paul. Some saint who is starting or already serving needs strength. God is sending us to strengthen someone. Will you go?

Sermon 4: Barnabas Shuns the Fame, Acts 11:25–26. One of the myths and misunderstandings of ministry is that one has to be first, out front, a favorite, very familiar, or regularly featured to be fruitful and to function in the fellowship. The truth is that one can be behind the scenes, in the background of the service, and still be a blessing to the saints. Barnabas is proof.

The Church at Antioch was blossoming and birthing believers. Barnabas discerned that the Church needed more than he, alone, could give, so he sought for the person who could meet the needs of the ministry and the members. "Then departed Barnabas to Tarsus, for to seek Saul" (v. 25). When Saul was brought to the Church at Antioch and put in leadership, Barnabas began to fade from the front and became a follower for the forwardness of the fellowship. The order in the listing of these two would soon reverse. We began by reading "Barnabas and Paul." Shortly, however, the listing will read "Paul and Barnabas," indicating Barnabas's shift in his role and responsibility. This is the standard, the stance, and the spirit of *the ideal Church member*: Barnabas.

What a great and gracious spirit to possess. Barnabas did not have to be in the command to contribute, the front to function, leadership to labor, the position to perform, or the spotlight to serve. Perhaps the most admirable quality in Barnabas is his complete willingness to take a back seat, to play second fiddle, and to stand in the shadows in service. Barnabas sought Saul, who could do for the people what he was not able to do. He recognized his limitations but did not limit the labor.

Sermon 5: Barnabas Stands by a Failure, Acts 15:36–41. This section of the Scripture tells of a sharp contention that separated the companionship of two of the strongest Christians. The separation was over one who had failed. Paul and Barnabas fell out over the failure of John Mark. They were meeting and making plans for their second missionary journey. Paul broached the subject with Barnabas, suggesting that they revisit the cities where they had previously preached the Word. When they reached the item on the agenda for suggestions of people to accompany them, Barnabas recommended John Mark. And that was the beginning of the dispute that divided the dynamic duo. Recall in Acts 13:13 when John Mark deserted them on the first missionary journey. The record is that when the ministry and the mission became hard, hot, heated, heavy, and harmful, John Mark left the work and returned home to Jerusalem. His name came up for recommendation to accompany them on the second missionary journey: "Barnabas determined to take with them John, whose surname was Mark. But Paul thought not good to take him with them, who departed from them from Pamphylia, and went not with them to the work. The contention was so sharp between them, that they departed asunder one from another" (Acts 15:37–39).

Since John Mark *did* redeem his character in these respects and a reconciliation took place between he and Paul, so cordial that the apostle expresses more than once the confidence he had in him and the value he set upon his services (Col. 4:10–11; 2 Tim. 4:11), it may seem that events showed Barnabas to be in the right and Paul too harsh and hasty in his judgment.

Mark was supremely fortunate that he had a friend like Barnabas. In the end, as we know, Mark became the man who redeemed himself. It may well have been the friendship of Barnabas that gave Mark back his self-respect and made him determined to make good. It is a great thing for a man to have someone who believes in him. Barnabas believed in Mark, and in the end Mark justified that belief. I thank God that failure is not final.

4. New Disciples Orientation Class

> The program to involve inactive Church members for every Church should be motivated by concern, love, and understanding. Every program should be person-centered, not Church-centered. The primary goal of the program should not be to increase attendance at Church activities but to increase a person's usefulness to Christ. Hopefully, it is the desired effect to see more activity in Church affairs, but it is more important to see a closer relationship to Jesus Christ. The Church, therefore, must be concerned with the person as a person, not as a prospect for attendance and finances. Every effort should be made to help people understand Christ's will for them and that He desires active involvement.[38]

What is most needful and helpful in assuring members' involvement is the New Disciples Orientation Class. In this class, the new member is taught the objectives of the Church, the obligations to the Church, the opportunities in the Church, and the operation of the Church. For this study, only the objectives and the introduction (the author's concept) are given.

New Disciples Orientation Class. In new member orientation, our Church is concerned with both new Christians and transfer members.

---

[38] Byrne, *Reclaiming Inactive Church Members,* 33.

Though needs may vary with different individuals, the basic objective of orientation is the same for all new members. It is to *lead each new member to make the commitment to Christ and the Church* and to strive diligently for Christian maturity as called for in the Word of God. More specifically, it is to achieve the following:

1. To help each new member understand and reaffirm his or her conversion experience and *his or her commitment to Christ and the Church.*
2. To help each new member understand and accept the *privileges and responsibilities* of membership in the Church.
3. To help each new member appropriate the resources of the Christian life and *become a growing part* of the Christian fellowship through *involvement in the life of the Church* during and beyond the orientation period.[39]

Introduction. As children, we were taught to beware of strangers. We were to be cautious, careful, and cognizant of them. We were told not to pick up strangers, not to go anywhere with them, and not to open the door to them. However, we are not so cautious, careful, and cognizant of strangers when it comes to the family of faith, the body of believers, and the Church of Christ. We allow strangers to have free course and full range without knowing their conversion, their cause, or their commitment.

If someone came to your home and met you for the first time, would your residence door become a register desk? Would your house become a hotel? Would your quaint become quarters? Would your keys to locks become keepsakes for lodgers? I do not think so. Then why do we do it with the Church? Someone comes down the aisle. We meet them for the first time and give them all the same rights and privileges of the Church as we have given all other members. But who is this individual?

---

39. James L. Sullivan, *Your Life, Your Church* (Nashville, TN: Convention Press, 1983), ix.

What are his or her intentions? What are his or her interests? What is the investment? We have no idea. Yet we offer everything to someone who has made no obligation to us. So, before we extend our Church, we need to earn a commitment. This is accomplished through New Disciple Orientation.

Orientation is that setting where the Church is introduced to an interested person and an interested person is introduced to the Church. Orientation is plowing the soil of ignorance and planting the seed of instruction. Orientation is the brochure for the believer, a compass for the Christian, education for the enrolled, a map for the member, and a salutation for the saint.

What is the interest of Christ? It is not the addition but the agreement. It is not the count but the commitment. It is not the increase but the involvement. What is the interest of the Church? The interest should be the same as Christ's. If it is, there should be requirements before rights, rules before registration, and relationship before responsibility.

At the Christian Union Primitive Baptist Church, where I am privileged to serve, the person who walks down the aisle to unite with our Church is not immediately received or recorded as a full member of the church. Each person goes through a process of membership.

1. Potential member—Coming with expression. According to *Webster's New Collegiate Dictionary*, *potential* is "expressing possibility" and "capable of developing into actuality."
2. Proven member—Completing the exercise. The potential member is placed in the orientation class. The class is nine weeks long and covers five lessons. During this time, potential members are being not only taught but tested as well. I ought to share with you that if they are committed, they will continue. If they are earnest, they will endure. If they are real, they will remain. If they are sincere, they will stay. However, if they drop out, discontinue, or disappear from the class or from the church, we are not bound to bestow any benefits. We have not contracted to consider any claims. We have not offered any

opportunities in our organization. We have not promised the possession of any privileges. In other words, if they leave, we have not lost, loaned, or loosed anything.

3. Presented member—Commended for enrollment. After coming with expression and completing the exercise, they are then commended for enrollment. For nine weeks, they have been influenced by our prerequisites, introduced to our precepts, instructed in our purpose, informed of our practices, and imposed with our potential, and they are still interested in being a part of our Church. At that time, they are received as members with all the rights and privileges of our Church.
4. Promising member—Continuance is expected. During the nine-week period, we try to target the talents, tendencies, trades, tools, and treasures of the potential member. Prior to presenting people to the church for membership, the chairman of the selected department and the president of the ministry are informed of the choice and are ready to receive them under their wings for further nurturing. So, after enrollment, they are provided with a prayer partner and a productive place. Therefore, the people who began as potential members become promising members. They are greeted by the Church, groomed in a class, and grouped with other Christians, which gives us a grip on their conduct and, for them, grounds for continuance. This is the opportunity, the optimism, and the obligation of orientation.

5. Supplying Prerequisites

Bob Welch, a speaker, author, award-winning columnist, and teacher who has served as an adjunct professor of journalism at the University of Oregon in Eugene, as quoted by Kenneth Gangel, said,

> Job descriptions should be reviewed annually by the employee and the administration. Any changes in job description should

> be reviewed by the employee and the administration. They should be agreed upon.
>
> Job description tells the applicant that your church is both organized and efficient. They provide conference, stability, accountability related to employee actions and interactions. They facilitate positive staff relationships making time spent on job descriptions time well spent."[40]

Who wants to volunteer for the unknown? Gather written descriptions for all ministry positions. Post them or hand them out.

6. Special Programs

I recognized that some members in the Church have talents and skills that can serve and save the members money. We put together a "Helping Hand Ministry Handbook." Each member was issued a survey to list his or her unofficial work. The talents and the skills were compiled and placed in categories along with members' contact information and distributed to Church members. Members in need of service were to contact a member before calling a professional. This would both serve members and save money. The service would solidify the membership, and the savings would support the ministry.

40. Kenneth O. Gangel, *Advanced Leadership and Administration*: ML503-MP01, Lecture 6 (Grand Rapids, MI: Institute of Theological Studies, 2009), quoting Bob Welch.

CONCLUSION

The problem of involvement is a problem of interest. When people are interested, they will be present, they will participate, and they will patronize. It is the belief of the author that the majority of the members on the Church roster are not not serious about their souls. Neither are they passionate about their spiritual progress. When an employee is always late for work, takes extended lunch hours, loafs on the job, and leaves early, it stands to reason that that employee is not interested in his or her job. When a student is consistently late for school, does not do homework or turn in assignments, and constantly distracts and disturbs the class, it stands to reason that that student is not interested in his or her education. Likewise, when a member does not attend the Word events of the Church, such as Church School, training classes, and Bible study, and is not involved in any ministry of the Church, it stands to reason that that member is not interested in spiritual growth. Where there is no interest, there will be no involvement. One of the greatest burdens borne by a pastor is being interested in people who are not interested in themselves.

The problem of involvement is the problem of importance. Everyone wants to feel needed. If members are never approached or never asked to attend a function or to perform a duty, they feel they are not needed. The truth of the matter is that each member has something we need. There is a gift, a talent, a skill, and an ability to contribute. Without them, the ministry is not complete. All members must be accepted, acknowledged, and appreciated if they are expected to be active.

The problem of involvement is the problem of identity. Presence and participation are the two main ways we identify the commitment, the conduct, and the contribution of a member. In Luke 15:3–7, when the sheep strayed away, the shepherd sought after that which was lost. He knew the identities of the sheep. When a member is missing in attendance and in activities, he or she should be identified, should be or should become the focus of outreach, and should be posted on the ministry's "Most Wanted" list.

The problem of involvement is the problem of information. The Church often operates on hearsay and gravitates to gossip. But if facts are needed, go to the source. The survey was the way to go to the people and ask them about their perceptions, their positions, and their problems. In asking, I learned that the lack of involvement has to do with the members' understanding or the lack of understanding of their Churches' image, instructions, infrastructure, intentions, or involvement in the community. Others are fearful of expectations, while others are fearful of being taxed. The Church must do a better job of defining the core values and the chief vocation of the Church.

The author has benefited from this work. It has strengthened his grip on the problem. Using the suggestions, services, and surveys, the author has witnessed an increase in commitments, cooperation, and contributions. My admonishment and advice is to have patience with the patient. There is healing for "paralysis in the pew." Rick Warren summarizes the message well:

> If you're not involved in any service or ministry, what excuse have you been using? Abraham was old, Jacob was insecure, Leah was unattractive, Joseph was abused, Moses stuttered, Gideon was poor, Samson was codependent, Rahab was immoral, David had an affair and all kinds of family problems, Elijah was suicidal, Jeremiah was depressed, Jonah was reluctant, Naomi was a widow, John the Baptist was eccentric to say the least, Peter was impulsive and hot-tempered, Martha worried a lot, The Samaritan had several failed marriages, Zacchaeus was

unpopular, Thomas had doubts, Paul had poor health, and Timothy was timid. That is quite a variety of misfits, but God used each of them in His service. He will use you, too, if you stop making excuses.[41]

---

41. Warren, *The Purpose Driven Life*, 233.

Appendix A

LETTER AND QUESTIONS FOR SURVEY

Dear Brother,

My name is Jeffrey T. Rainey. I am presently enrolled at Faith Evangelical College and Seminary based in Tacoma, Washington. I am in the process of writing my dissertation as a requirement of the Doctor of Ministry program. My dissertation is titled: "Paralysis in the Pew." To help me complete this project, I am asking for your help by giving this survey to a core group within your congregation. Upon their completion, you may do a summary report of the data received from their responses. The surveys will be included as a part of my project, and you and your congregation will be acknowledged and credited for your contribution.

I thank you deeply in advance for your assistance with this assignment.

Questions for Survey

1. What is your age?
   - o 1–11 years
   - o 12–17 years
   - o 18–25 years
   - o 26–40 years
   - o 41–60 years
   - o 61 or more

2. What is your gender?
   - o Male
   - o Female

3. How long have you been a member of your current Church?
   - o 0–5 years
   - o 6–10 years
   - o 11 or more years

4. What is the extent of your involvement?
   - o Low
   - o Moderate
   - o High
   - o Nonexistent

5. Do you currently serve in a leadership role?
   - o No
   - o Yes

6. How would you generally describe your congregation?
   - o Evangelistic
   - o (Sunday) worship centered
   - o Missions oriented
   - o Community linked by shared/common culture

7. How would you describe the level of stress experienced by your core group of leaders due to various demands of ministry?
   - o Nonexistent
   - o Low
   - o Moderate
   - o High

8. How would you describe the distribution of tasks within your congregation?
   - o 80/20 (80% watching/20% working)
   - o 50/50 (50% watching/50% working)
   - o 20/80 (20% watching/80% working)

9. How does low participation affect the level of stress among the core group leaders? What amount of stress does low participation have upon the stress levels of core group leaders?
   - o None
   - o Low
   - o Moderate
   - o High

10. Are the ministries of your Church able to accommodate the abilities, the gifts, and the talents of the membership?
    - o Yes
    - o No
    - o I don't know

11. Does the Church provide an atmosphere that encourages membership involvement?
    - o Yes
    - o No
    - o I don't know

12. Are there incentives and/or information made available for increased participation? What is the current level of effort made by the leadership to engage all members in meaningful ministry?
    - o Low
    - o Medium
    - o High
    - o I don't know

13. Does your Church have a mission and vision statement?
    - o Yes
    - o No
    - o I don't know

14. Is there a mechanism within your Church for communicating the mission vision and goals of your Church?
    - o Yes
    - o No
    - o I don't know

15. Do you sense that the members care about their Church image in the community?
    - o Yes
    - o No
    - o Haven't thought about it

BIBLIOGRAPHY

Anthony, Michael J. *The Effective Church Board: A Handbook for Mentoring and Training Servant Leaders*. Eugene, OR: Wipf and Stock Publishers, 2000.

Baxter, J. R., and Lucie E. Campbell. "He'll Understand and Say Well Done," *Lyrics Universal Music Publishing Group*. http://www.metrolyrics.com/hell-understand-and-say-well-done-lyrics-ferlin-husky.html

Byrne, Herbert W. *Reclaiming Inactive Church Members*. Bloomington, IL: Trafford Publishing, 2006.

Dover, Mark. *What Is a Healthy Church?* (Wheaton, IL: Crossway Publishing, 2007), 97.

Gangel, Kenneth O. *Advanced Leadership and Administration*. ML503-MP01 Lecture 6. Grand Rapids, MI: Institute of Theological Studies, 2009.

"How to Reactivate Your Inactive Church Members." *LifeWay.com*. http://www.lifeway.com/Article/How-to-reactivate-your-inactive-church-members

Jones, Mark S. *Reclaiming Inactive Church Members*. Nashville, TN: Broadman Press, 1988.

Kouzes, James M., and Barry Z. Posner. *The Leadership Challenge*. San Francisco: Jossey-Bass, 2007.

Lawless, Chuck, and Thom S. Rainer. *Membership Matters: Insights from Effective Churches on New Member Classes and Assimilation*. Grand Rapids, MI: Zondervan, 2005.

Leeman, Jonathan. *Church Membership*. Wheaton, IL: Crossway Publishing, 2012

Liddell, Henry George and Robert Scott. "παράλυσις" *A Greek-English Lexicon*. (Oxford: Clarendon Press on Perseus, 1940).

Malphurs, Aubrey. *Advanced Strategic Planning*. Grand Rapids, MI: Baker Books, 2005.

Maxwell, John C. *The 21 Indispensable Qualities of a Leader*. Nashville, TN: Thomas Nelson Press, 1999.

McIntosh, Gary, and Glen Martin. *Finding Them, Keeping Them: Effective Strategies for Evangelism and Assimilation in the Local Church*. Nashville, TN: Broadman Press, 1992.

Nash, Donald H. *Practical New Testament Word Studies*. Christian Restoration Association, 1982.

Pattison, Thomas Harwood. *The Making of a Sermon*. Whitefish, MT: Kessinger Publishing, LLC, 2009.

Peterson, Eugene H. *Run with the Horses*: *The Quest for Life at Its Best* (Downers Grove, IL: InterVarsity Press, 1983), 38.

Practical Word Studies in the New Testament, Page 1813 Copyright © 1998, by Alpha-Omega Ministries, Inc. All rights reserved. Database © 2014 WORD*search*.

Rainer, Thom S. *I Am A Church Member: Discovering the Attitude that Makes the Difference*. Nashville, TN: B & H Publishing Group, 2013.

Reese, Michael E. "Expository Preaching I." Birmingham Theological Seminary. Birmingham, AL. http://birminghamseminary.org/wp-content/uploads/2012/03/PT5722-Reese.pdf

Richardson, Ronald W. *Creating a Healthier Church: Family Systems Theory, Leadership, and Congregational Life*. Minneapolis, MN: Fortress Press, 1996.

Rigden, Jonathan. "How to Build Up Motivation and Encouragement in Church Members." *eHow.com*. http://www.ehow.com/how_7828877_build-motivation-encouragement-church-members.html

Schultz, Thom, and Joani Schultz. *Why Nobody Wants to Go to Church Anymore*. Loveland, CO: Group Publishing, 2013.

Sullivan, James L. *Your Life, Your Church*. Nashville, TN: Convention Press, 1983.

Warren, Rick. *The Purpose Driven Life: What on Earth Am I Here For?* Grand Rapids, MI: Zondervan, 2002.

Williams, Dennis E., and Kenneth O. Gangel. *Volunteers for Today's Church: How to Recruit and Retain Workers*. Eugene, OR: Wipf and Stock Publishers, 2004.

Printed in the United States
By Bookmasters